Faith
on
Earth?

Lou Poumakis' *Faith on Earth?* is clear in its language, cogent in its presentation, and bold in its challenge to Christians to obey God's laws. Here and there, it's even rather startling. The reader will probably find himself asking, probably more than once, "Why didn't I think of that?"

LEE DUIGON

Contributing Editor to the Chalcedon Foundation's *Faith for All of Life magazine*, and author of the *Bell Mountain Series* of novels

Faith
on Earth?

When the Son of man cometh,
shall he find Faith on Earth?

(Luke 18:8)

Lou Poumakis

7th *Millennium*

Ventura, California
2013

Faith on Earth?

When the Son of man cometh,
shall he find faith on earth? (Luke 18:8)

by Lou Poumakis

Copyright ©2013 by Eleuthere (Lou) Poumakis

International Standard Book Number: 978-0-9831957-8-8
Library of Congress Control Number: 2013934608

Cover Photo: NASA Image
Copyright © 123RF Stock Photos
Used by Permission.

Printed in the United States of America.

Published by

AN IMPRINT OF

Nordskog Publishing, Inc.
2716 Sailor Ave., Ventura, California 93001, USA
1-805-642-2070 • 1-805-276-5129

www.NordskogPublishing.com

MEMBER

Christian Small Publishers Association

TABLE OF CONTENTS

INTRODUCTION

"NEVERTHELESS when the Son of man cometh, shall he find faith on the earth?" (Luke 18:8). These words from the Lord come at the end of a parable about a widow's prayer for deliverance.[1] They seem out of place, a cryptic remark disconnected from the subject at hand. But there it is and, when we look at the history of the Christian faith, we can see there is cause for concern. There certainly could have been no doubt on the Lord's part as to the outcome but He doesn't indulge in asking idle questions. There is a strong implication here that says: first, man bears responsibility for the maintenance of the faith; and, second, the presence or absence of faith on earth when He returns depends on man. As we shall see, Christ has given His people much more responsibility than most Christians would acknowledge today. Without denying God's sovereign control over all things, we can say that Christianity has no life of its own; its continuance and survival depends on Christians who make it what it is.

There was a time, really not so long ago, when Christianity was the dominant faith in the Western world. It thrived in Europe, Australia, South Africa, and the Americas. In the Colonial era until well after the War of Independence, Christianity was virtually the only religion in America. During this period the Christian faith was central to the life of virtually

---

1 For a thorough exposition of this passage see: R. J. Rushdoony, *Salvation and Godly Rule*, Vallecito, CA: Ross House Books, 1983, 413–417.

1

the entire population.[2] Christianity is still the largest of the world's religions. Its numbers, particularly in the West, may not have changed greatly, but its influence on the cultures of the world has diminished markedly. Indeed, it is evident to the most casual observer that Christian influence in the Western world is now only a very small fraction of what it once was. Christianity has changed; it no longer has the cultural vitality it once displayed. When we look at the worldviews espoused and demonstrated by most of the leaders and educators of the Western world, the true extent of the degradation of Christian influence can be better assessed.

The challenges to Christianity today are greater than ever before. The anti-Christian forces arrayed against it and seeking its demise are powerful and deeply entrenched. They either control directly or at least are able to strongly influence every significant world power and are moving inexorably toward a socialistic and atheistic one-world government. What is needed to prevent their plunging the world into an age of abysmal darkness and to preserve or regain individual freedom is a restoration of Christian credibility and vitality. This will not be accomplished without a major sea change in thought and deed within the ranks of Christianity. But before reasonable and effective action can be taken, we need to understand the current situation, and, even more importantly, how we got here. The following is an attempt to explore, in very much an overview fashion, what the changes were, why they took place, and what will be needed to recover the ground that has been lost.

The author of this work does not claim originality for much of the content. He draws heavily from the lifelong works of Cornelius Van Til and R. J. Rushdoony who have made extensive contributions toward the advancement and development of Biblical understanding—the former having laid the theological and philosophical basis for the latter's writing on a broad range of subjects pertaining to the Christian faith and its relationship to culture. The works of both are well worth further study.

There is no intent in this work to produce a thorough analysis comprehending every detail of each point raised. It is rather to provide an outline of what is today an important aspect of the Christian faith that is

---

2 Winthrop S. Hudson. *Religion in America*, 4th ed. New York: Macmillan Publishing Co., 1987, 13–18.

not addressed in most Christian books or theological material. It is the author's hope that the reader will be sufficiently motivated to investigate further.

The ideas contained herein are not likely to gain immediate widespread acceptance; today's church is not yet ready for strong medicine. But there is a growing remnant who are aware that something is seriously wrong in society and that many of the churches are either part of the problem or just not relevant to a solution. The time is coming though, perhaps fairly soon, when it will become obvious to many more true believers that their leaders have let them down and have thereby brought about calamitous changes in America and the rest of the world. It is hoped that this work will lead some of the faithful to a better grasp of Christian responsibility and the scope of Scripture, particularly for application to life in this world and the future it promises—in time and in history.

PART ONE

THE

FAITH

1
ORIGINS

When and where did Christianity originate? What are its roots? How old is the faith that we now call the Christian Faith? These questions go beyond a desire merely to satisfy curiosity. How they are answered affects our basic understanding of Christianity itself and what it means to be a Christian. A right understanding of the historical origins of a belief system often sheds much light on the nature and applicability of the teachings of that system. It's important that any study of the faith begin with a correct view of its origins. The common belief today is that Christianity originated with the coming of Christ and is about 2,000 years old. What we now know as Judaism claims origination from Abraham in ca. 2000 BC, which makes it almost twice as old. Both Christianity and Judaism appeal to Holy Scripture—the Word of the Creator God—so one must go there to gain a better understanding of their origins.

OLD TESTAMENT FAITH AND CHRISTIANITY

In John 5:45–47 we read Jesus' statement that Moses was writing of Him in Deuteronomy 18:15, but the leaders of the Jews did not believe Him. In John 7:19 He told them that none of them kept God's law. In many other passages, Christ castigates the Pharisees for their failure to follow Moses and believe in the Messiah, of whom he wrote (see Matt. 23:13-35; Mark 7:10-12, 12:26-27; John 7:19, 22-24). The faith that Christ was defending at this time, the faith that Moses had but the

Pharisees apparently did not have, was faith in Him, faith in the Christ, the second Person of the Triune God.[3] This faith in the Person of Christ is what characterizes Christianity. We speak of it today as being the Christian Faith.

Moses, of course, wrote the first five books of the Old Testament, known in Biblical terms as the Law. Since Jesus told us Moses was speaking of Him, this tells us that Christ is in and behind the Old Testament Law (see John 5:39; Matt. 5:17-19). Indeed, references to Christ are not limited to Moses but can be found throughout the Old Testament. Paul tells us that Abraham, whom God chose to be the patriarch of ancient Israel, held to that same faith and therefore was the father of all Christian believers (see Rom. 4:1-3, 9, 12, 13, 16; Gal. 3:29). The prophets, some of the kings, and many other Old Testament saints held to this faith in Christ (Heb. 11). The Israelites of Moses' day looked forward to the coming of the Messiah, the Anointed One, to whom all the sacrifices offered by the Israelites pointed.

These verses make it clear that ancient Israel held to the same faith as do Christians today, faith in the Christ, the second person of the Holy Trinity. The difference, of course, was in perspective. Today we look back to the incarnation. For the ancients, the Christ was yet to come and the exact nature of His coming was not as clear to them as it is to us today. The sacrificial system God gave Israel was instituted to keep the faithful on track. It offset this lack of clarity by demonstrating the seriousness of sin and the need for the shedding of blood as its remission (Heb. 9:22). The sacrifices were necessary then but, if continued today, would represent a denial of Christ's final sacrifice (Heb. 10:9-14). So, with this understanding of the temporary expediency of the sacrificial system as an exception, there does not appear to be any essential difference between the religion of ancient Israel and Christianity. Both revered the same God, both acknowledged the truth of His word—which at that time was limited to the

---

3 The concept of the Triune God is evident from the Hebrew language which has dual and plural forms. The name for God in Genesis 1:1, "In the beginning God [*Elohim*, plural of at least three persons, not singular or dual] created" [singular verb form in Hebrew as in He (singular) created] reveals both the plurality and singularity of the nature of God. (See Neil Cullan McKinlay, *From Mason to Minister*, Ventura, CA: Nordskog Publishing, 2011, 83.) And in Genesis 1:26 God refers to Himself in the plural when He says, "Let us make man in our image...."

Old Testament—and both looked to the Son as Savior.

For a variety of reasons, this early faith degraded over the centuries. But even as late as at the time of Christ's birth, there were still some of the faithful in Israel that did believe and recognized Jesus as the Messiah (see Luke 2:25–34). The inventions of the priests and religious leaders corrupted the faith to such an extent that most did not recognize their Messiah when He came. These religious leaders refused to listen to His words of correction and, finally, as was prophesied in the Scriptures, they had Him crucified.

By this time, the transition of the religion of national Israel away from the true faith to rabbinic Judaism was well advanced. With the resurrection of Christ and the work of the Apostles, that true faith was reborn in Christianity—first among the Jews, and then in the Gentile world. We read in the New Testament of thousands of Jews including many priests that believed in Christ.

> Then they that gladly received his word were baptized: and the same day there were added unto them about three thousand souls. (Acts 2:41)

> Howbeit many of them which heard the word believed; and the number of the men was about five thousand. (Acts 4:4)

> And the word of God increased; and the number of the disciples multiplied in Jerusalem greatly; and a great company of the priests were obedient to the faith. (Acts 6:7)

> And when they heard it, they glorified the Lord, and said unto him, Thou seest, brother, how many thousands of Jews there are which believe; and they are all zealous of the law: (Acts 21:20)

These were not converts in the true sense of the word; they merely returned to the faith of their fathers and acknowledged Christ as their Messiah.

Paul tells us that the children of the flesh are not necessarily the children of God, and he refers to Christian believers as "the Israel of God" (see Rom. 9:6; Gal. 6:15–16). Indeed, Christianity has always been based on faith; its heritage follows a faith-line, rather than a blood-line. The

Pharisees taught that God favored the Jews because of their lineage from Abraham through Isaac to Jacob, but it was never that. It was always the faith of the people as expressed in their obedience to God that made them His people and resulted in His blessing. Regardless of race, national origin, church, or family background, anyone who places his faith in Christ, is a Christian. This was as true in ancient Israel as it is today.

The idea that the Christian faith was alive and well more than a thousand years before Jesus was born may sound strange to modern ears. But what is Christianity other than faith in the true God, the God of Abraham, Isaac, and Jacob? And wasn't ancient Israel founded on just that faith? Consider the confession the apostle Paul made before the Roman governor Felix:

> But this I confess unto thee, that after the way which they call heresy, so worship I the God of my fathers, believing all things which are written in the law and in the prophets. (Acts 24:14)

Paul is defending here the Christian faith—which the Jewish leaders were calling heresy—as being the logical continuity of the ancient faith found in the law and the prophets (the Old Testament Scriptures). Paul was a Jew, a learned Pharisee; he studied under Gamaliel, a descendant of Hillel, and knew that faith in great detail. When he says that Christianity is not something new but is the true faith of ancient Israel, we should take notice. More significantly, these are not just the words of the man Paul. They are the inspired words of Holy Scripture, which cannot be set aside.

Furthermore, to assert that faith in ancient Israel was not the same as Christian faith is to say that the God of the Old Testament is not the same God as the God of the New Testament (see Heb. 13:8). It is, in effect, to erroneously ignore the Old Testament as part of the Bible. But this is impossible because the Bible is a unified entity; the two testaments are interwoven much too tightly together to be separated without destroying the new and rendering the old unintelligible.[4]

---

4 For an in-depth study of the unity of the Old and New Testaments, see: Charles D. Provan, *The Church Is Israel Now.* Vallecito, CA: Ross House Books, 1987.

EARLIER FAITH

To return to the question of timing, one can look in the Ancient Near East and in Early Dynastic Egypt and find many religions that are even earlier than Moses (ca. 1450 BC). But we can actually date the origin of the Biblical faith much earlier. After Adam and Eve sinned in the Garden, God promised he would send His Son (the seed of the woman) who would crush Satan's head (see Gen. 3:15). Later, in the godly line following Seth, men began to "call upon the name of the LORD" (Gen. 4:26). The word LORD in this instance is a reference to the true God—Father, Son, and Holy Spirit—the God of the whole Bible. It is very likely they looked forward to the coming of the seed of the woman as God promised. We can conclude then that the line of Seth shared, at least to some extent, what is today, the Christian faith.

The true faith, though, actually existed even earlier; it is the faith that prevailed prior to the Fall where we read that God spoke with Adam in the Garden (see Gen. 2:16-17, 28-29; 3:8) and Adam was obedient to Him. At that time, Adam and Eve worshipped the true God: Father, Son, and Holy Spirit, the God of the whole Bible. Christ's atonement on the cross was yet future at this time but it was still inherent in their worship and faith.

Christianity is not merely an addition to, or an offshoot of, Judaism; it is the oldest religion in the world. It is the embodiment of God's eternal plan for what man should believe and how he should worship and has a continuity that extends throughout all of history. Without this perspective, we lose or misunderstand much of what Scripture says about the faith. Christianity is not a Johnny-come-lately religion. It goes all the way back to Adam and Eve and it cannot be properly understood without that context.

HUMANISM

The religion that has roots almost as old as Christianity is humanism. It dates from the Fall itself when Eve and then Adam, acting in accordance with the serpent's lie, decided to be their own gods (Gen. 3:5). This was a definite change in religion; they worshipped new gods (themselves) and had a new faith—a faith in Satan's word instead of God's word. Most humanists today insist that they are not religious, and, unlike Christians or others who believe in God, they believe in science. They define religion as belief in a god but the correct definition is "a set of beliefs concerning the cause, nature, and purpose of the universe."[5] Humanists believe that the universe had no purpose or design and came into being entirely by accident. This certainly cannot be empirically proven and is, therefore, a belief—a religious belief. Some tenets of this faith are the Big Bang, abiogenesis (life arising spontaneously from non-life), and Darwinian evolution. That humanism is a religion is affirmed by Humanist Manifesto I, which begins:

> First: Religious humanists regard the universe as self-existing and not created.

> Second: Humanism believes that man is a part of nature and that he has emerged as the result of a continuous process.[6]

This is humanism in its modern form. (Humanism can be defined in a broad sense where it takes many forms: eastern mysticism, Hinduism, Confucianism, and including Islam that copied the Bible yet is a man-made false religion that opposes the true God of the Bible, etc., as well as in the more narrow, modern sense of atheism and agnosticism.) All are based on man's word and man's ideas of God. All are forms of idolatry that worship the creature rather than the Creator.

So upon further examination we can see that, from the Christian point of view, elements of Christianity and humanism are the basic constituents of all the world's religions. All others are some combination or variant of these two. Christianity represents faith in God's word, and humanism on the other hand represents faith in man's word. This, then, is the key: Who is it that is speaking in these religious documents? Is it God or man? The Bible not only claims to be the absolute word of God, but in it God Himself speaks: "All Scripture is given by inspiration of God" (see 2 Tim. 3:16). All others are clearly man-made documents containing man's opinions as to origins, purpose, and ethics.

---

5 http://dictionary.reference.com/browse/religion

6 Copyright 1933 by New Humanist (newhumanist.org.uk) and 1973 by American Humanist Association (americanhumanist.org).

There are, then, only two basic religions: belief in the God of the Bible (Christianity) or belief in man (humanism). Most other religions contain only vestiges of the true faith as carried by Noah's family into the post-flood world where it scattered into variant expressions. But as one would expect, these have diverged widely as man's ideas were introduced over the centuries and now bear little resemblance to God's word.

It is also true that neither Biblical faith nor humanism is practiced in a pure sense anywhere. Although they might not like to admit it, human-ists cannot help but have a great deal of Christian influence (God's word) in the philosophy they live by and, consequently, their faith. Humanistic scientists, for example, assume that their experiments and discoveries have meaning and purpose and that they fit into an orderly, rather than chaotic, universe. There is no basis for such a view other than in the Bible.[7] Likewise, as we shall see in what follows, Christians have imbibed considerable quantities of humanism (man's word) in both their theology and their practice. Many of the troubles of mankind throughout his-tory can be traced to the confusion caused by the intermixing of these two faiths.

---

7 There is much evidence in support of the truth of the Christian faith but the most powerful argument (developed and documented by Cornelius Van Til) is that without the creative and continuing providential work of the Triune God whom we find only in the Bible, there could be no order in the universe. Because meaning is dependent on order, this would render all facts meaningless and human knowledge itself would be impossible. See: Cornelius Van Til, *The Defense of the Faith*. Philadelphia: Presbyterian and Reformed Publishing Co., 1967, 31–46.

2

PROGRESS

THE worldwide expansion of the Christian faith began with the resurrection of Jesus Christ and the work of the twelve apostles in the Mediterranean area during the Roman Empire. It took hold so vigorously that within the short space of three centuries, it was well on its way toward becoming the dominant faith of the Empire.

For a thousand years following, it retained that position of dominance in the Western world. History knows Europe in that time as "Christendom." Kings and emperors, whether actually Christian believers or not, were required to assent to the faith if they wanted to retain their authority. Almost the entire population believed in God and assented to the Apostles' Creed as gospel truth. Kings or rulers that refused to submit publicly to Christ as King of kings and LORD of lords did not receive the support they needed from the general population.

Christianity was not only a faith people held in their hearts, a faith that gave them comfort in difficult times or a promise of better times to come in the afterlife, it was a faith that determined the nature of the culture in which it lived. Even though it was almost always practiced very imperfectly, it was a vital faith, one that did not tolerate or compromise with foreign or competing religions in any aspect of public life. The generally accepted belief during those times was that Christianity would become the religion of the whole world, that all peoples on earth would eventually come to the true faith and would receive the blessings that accompanied life in a Christian culture. Many—even though they were acting outside the church, notably the Explorers, Columbus, Magellan, Cortez, De Gama, and others—worked to spread the Gospel to other nations and cultures. Christianity in that period was an optimistic faith. The church believed that it would eventually stand alone, having displaced all its false-faith competitors.

The English Puritans carried this faith to Colonial America and formed the foundation of this country's laws and way of life. Early Americans held to the hope and faith of the early church. They believed that America was a new land of Canaan and they believed themselves the new Israel of prophecy, where the true Gospel would be nurtured and propagated— first throughout America and then to the rest of the world. Americans believed that God gave them that work to do as a people and as a nation. Jonathan Edwards and other writers in that period wrote extensively of their faith in the eventual victory of Christianity over every other religion in the whole world.[8]

These ideas held sway with most of the population into the nineteenth century. R. L. Dabney, a post-Civil-War-era Presbyterian theologian, speaking to a recent rise in opposition to the Christian faith, said,

> The country is sprinkled all over with infidels.... They may keep their hostility to themselves in the main; because Christianity now "walks in her silver slippers"; but they are not the less steeled [less set] against all saving impressions of the truth.[9]

Dabney recognized that unbelief was growing but also observed that these opponents of the faith were unable to speak out against the church because, as recently as late in the nineteenth century, Christianity reigned supreme in America. She "walks in her silver slippers."

The Founding Fathers that drew up the Constitution—along with the population at large—generally saw the Bible as the basic law book, the Constitution being merely a procedural document that ordered such

---

8 Iain H. Murray, *Jonathan Edwards: A New Biography*, Edinburgh: The Banner of Truth Trust, 1987.

9 Robert L. Dabney, *Discussions, Volume I: Theological and Evangelical*, 1890. Harrisonburg, VA: Sprinkle Publications, 1982, 572–73.

things as the scope and structure of civil government and the terms of office for elected officials. Well into the nineteenth century, judges in courtrooms, when ready to sentence offenders found guilty by a jury, typically would read a passage of Scripture, one pertinent to the case, before passing judgment. This action demonstrated their reliance on the Bible and its relevance to judicial decisions.[10] The Christian faith and the Bible dominated the culture and laws of early America.

---

10 R. J. Rushdoony, *Law and Liberty*. Vallecito, CA: Ross House Books, 1984, 2009, 112.

3

REGRESS

SADLY, this happy state of affairs did not survive to the present day. In Europe, the church hierarchy grew more and more corrupt as time passed. This led to the Italian Renaissance, which, partially as a reaction against an extremely corrupt church, reintroduced earlier humanistic ideas that conflicted with Christian thought. These foreign ideas were later carried even further by the French Enlightenment and gradually took root in the European intellectual community.

The common people held to the faith much longer, but by the nineteenth century, Europe was no longer Christendom. Earlier, the Dutch, with help from the English, fought against Spain to save Dutch Protestants from being exterminated by the Inquisition. In an attempt to wipe out Protestantism, the Spanish army under Fernando Alvarez de Toledo, the Duke of Alva, slaughtered huge numbers of men, women, and children before the Dutch prevailed and finally won their freedom. This sacrifice brought religious freedom to the Netherlands where it survived for centuries. Sadly though, there is now very little Christianity remaining in that once strongly Christian nation. Europe today is largely a godless society where church-going Christians are very much in the minority.[11] Its native

---

11 Collin Hansen, "Europe's Past Is Today's Hope," *Christianity Today*, October 2009. Carol Stream, IL: Christianity Today International. http://www.christianitytoday.com/ct/2009/octoberweb-only/140-11-0.html.

population is declining rapidly, with an Islamic population seemingly in the process of replacing it. The consensus today is that if the present trend continues, by the end of the twenty-first century, Europe will be Muslim Europe, very likely ruled by Sharia law.

America, isolated by two oceans, has held on longer. Millions of Americans still go to church on Sundays but Christianity barely influences, much less controls, the culture. American Christianity, as far as its impact on the culture at large is concerned, is now in serious decline. Bibles are not permitted in public schools, and students may not mention God, Christ, or Jesus; these have become forbidden words. Babies are legally put to death before or during the birth process at the whim of the mother. Pornography and homosexuality are culturally acceptable and may not be challenged under penalty of law.

Americans go to church but America's laws are, in practice, no longer Christian. The laws of a nation reflect the true cultural and religious standards of that country. American Christians by default have given over control of the culture to non-Christians. This is quite evident from the most cursory examination of our more recently enacted laws, the entertainment media, education, the family, and almost any metric that can be employed to measure the change in publicly accepted values over the past several decades. At one time, Bible-believing Christians had almost total control of the government; yet, by the end of the twentieth century, they had virtually lost it all and now have little influence in public affairs. Tens of millions of babies have been killed since 1973 (*Roe v. Wade*), and the slaughter continues. The religion of humanism has, in effect, taken virtually total control of both the European and American cultures.

The track record of Christianity, then, has been one of rapid initial growth followed by a long period during which it was the center of cultural thought and leadership followed by a recent decline in influence that is now accelerating at an alarming rate. The loss of faith is especially notable today in Europe and among American intellectuals. If this trend continues, America will lose its faith just as Europe already has. The Christian faith can hardly be sustained in an environment where an aberrant belief-system is inculcated into the youth in their schools and where the entire information and entertainment media reflect and promulgate that same belief system.

Christians have put up token resistance against these incursions but their hearts were not in it. Their focus was on getting through this life and into the glorious future that awaits them in the next. Even today, most Christian leaders put far more effort into church attendance, foreign missions, and evangelism than into real culture-impacting activities. This is not to say that these are unimportant. It's just that while this focus is being maintained, culturally important issues such as government control of education, the filth that is called entertainment, and the godlessness of our leaders are being largely neglected. Home schooling has been a reaction against the government schools' involvement in religious training but, if Christians remain as passive as they are today, how long will home schooling be permitted to exist as an option?

The religion of humanism, the idea that there is nothing and no one above man, that man is the ultimate determiner of all things, has replaced Christianity as the dominant religion of the Western world. Even though most Westerners still call themselves Christians, the leadership and the power elite are mostly practicing humanists and many are actively anti-Christian.

So that's where things stand as of today, but is there no remedy? Is Christianity destined to die a slow death and, if not to fade out altogether, to remain a sub-culture with a bare remnant holding to the faith? Will Christ find faith on earth when He returns? To answer these questions, we need to look at what God tells us in His word and what the Bible has to say about the significance of the Christian faith and mankind's responsibilities in this world.

PART TWO

HOW
WE
GOT
HERE

B EFORE we can hope to see a permanent and true Christian culture established, we need to understand why Christianity has transitioned from a dynamic, culture-determining force to what today amounts to a large but aging, past-oriented, less-and-less relevant social influence. Why has this change taken place, and why is Christianity clearly on its way to becoming an impotent, insignificant subculture? Surely if we had followed God's instructions faithfully this could not have happened. We would not have lost the ground we had gained—often at a terrible price— if we had remained obedient to God. It may be that there are problems with what we have believed and put into practice. We should review our current understanding of God's word with a critical eye to see whether or not we've been misled or somehow strayed from a correct perception of God's directions and commandments.

The essence of this book's thesis is:

1. God is in control of whatever happens on earth.

2. God rewards obedience with blessings and disobedience with curses.

3. Obedience to God must be TOTAL—without restrictions or exceptions.

4. Christians have not obeyed and actually have knowingly discarded many of God's commandments.

5. Christianity has faltered because God is chastising his people for their disobedience.

6. God's blessing will be restored and the Christian faith will recover when Christians begin to obey ALL of God's commandments.[12]

The remainder of this work is presented in the spirit of explanation and support of this assessment.

---

12 The sacrificial laws were pointers to Christ. Animal sacrifices, if performed today, would be a denial of His final sacrifice. See the section under "God's Law, Objections: The Sacrificial System," pp. 63–66.

4

GOD IN CONTROL

EVERYTHING begins with God. He is the only being without a beginning or end, and He is the only source and sustainer of all that exists. As the Infinite Creator, He is the ultimate environment in which everything else—the entire universe—exists. He inhabits all of His creation, yet exists apart from it.

As finite creatures, it is very difficult for us to grasp the concept of infinity and we tend to remake God into something we can visualize more readily. This was very obvious with the pagan panoply of Greek and Roman gods that were just a little larger and a little more powerful than men, and who were governed by their emotions and appetites, much like men. It is less obvious among most Christians today, but the tendency to think of God as a fellow resident within the universe is still quite prevalent. The danger inherent in this kind of thinking is that it detracts from the reality of God's utter and complete independence of anything outside of Himself, especially man. This leads to the idea that in some way God needs man and is to some extent at man's mercy. Nothing could be further from the truth.

One of God's attributes is His aseity (self-originated existence): He is the "I Am," the only absolutely independent, completely self-determining being. We are all dependent to one degree or another on many things, but God is not so constrained. He does His will in all the earth and nothing can thwart His plans (see Isa. 46:9–10). This majestic, almighty, all-knowing, and absolutely perfect being decided to create this universe for His own profound and incomprehensible purposes. He created the earth and all that's in it in accordance with His will. He directs all events—including man's activities—to accomplish these purposes. God not only created but also sustains all of His creation; Scripture is very clear on this (see Gen. 50:20; Ps. 104:27–29; Isa. 44:6).

If we want to understand history and what is transpiring in the world, we must take what God has said into serious consideration. To not do so is to disregard the most significant factor in the equation; it is to ignore the elephant in the room. God directs the affairs of men to accomplish His own ends and purposes. This is not to affirm fatalism. Man's actions are significant and have consequences, but they do not sum up the totality of action and reaction, of cause and effect. In order to get a grasp of why events have proceeded the way they have in history, we must begin with God and God's overriding plan and purpose.

We are most fortunate in that God has not been silent in this regard. He has very clearly delineated His plan for this world and man as a central player in it. God created man and placed him in this world to live in peace and glorify Him in all we do. But He didn't stop there; He also gave us very clear and comprehensive directions as to how to do so. We cannot comprehend His total purpose but, with some effort, we can come to appreciate our responsibilities within that purpose.

THE BIBLE

The source and definition of Christianity is the Bible. Scripture is not merely a record of historical events, nor is it just a record of revelational events. It is revelation itself. It is God speaking to man. Without continual grounding and guidance from the Bible, Christianity loses its focal point and diverges in accordance with any popular notion that may arise. Each individual invents his own version of truth and all become idolaters. Any diminution of the authority of Scripture is a step in this direction and those that propose such are enemies of God.

Thus, as the written communication of the Creator to His creatures, the Bible is, and must be, inerrant in every respect. The presence of a single error in a book that purports to be the word of an omnipotent, omniscient, and omnipresent God would invalidate everything it says.

22

If any word from God were false, then God Himself would be false and could not be trusted in anything He said. The Bible would then become a fallible word and Christianity would fall to the ground. Without a sure and certain word from God, there can be no Christianity. Christians have for two millennia maintained that the words of Scripture (in the original manuscripts) were inspired by God (God-breathed) (2 Tim. 3:16) and then preserved by God's providence through all the centuries since. God spoke through the prophets and the apostles, but He didn't stop there. He caused His words to be put into written form and then to be preserved so that each generation is faced with its responsibilities toward God. Even the poorest translations still reflect the essential elements of those responsibilities. All that follows here assumes that the Bible, from cover to cover, is true and infallibly correct in all it states.

Further, the Bible cannot be looked upon as merely a disjointed collection of information that can be mined for gems of knowledge. It is an integrated, coherent whole—an instruction manual written by the Creator for His creatures. It tells a single story, the center of which is the Son of God, the Messiah. His incarnation and appearance in history is first prophesied at the beginning of history in the third chapter of Genesis; and, when not in the forefront, He is always behind the scenes throughout the Old and New Testaments.

When taken as merely one of many information sources, the Bible becomes a tool in man's hands to serve his purposes. But the Bible was given to us to show us God's purposes, not as an instrument to further our own ends. We miss a great deal of what it has to say to us when we lose sight of this principle of coherence contained within its pages and of the fact that this is God's book written to communicate His purposes to His creatures.

Another common failing is to view the Bible as a book of instructions related primarily to eternal salvation as opposed to life in this world. For many today, the promises found in the Bible are not seen as particularly relevant to this world. Salvation is seen entirely as salvation from hell's fire and is equated with eternal life. But eternal life is not something that begins after death. It begins now, in this life, and carries with it the responsibilities God has placed upon His chosen people. Among Christians today, there is little thought given to salvation from the evils of this present world, much less the salvation of nations as Christ spoke of just prior to His ascension (Matt. 28:18–20). This next-life orientation of Christian thought is what lies behind much of the increasing loss of Christian influence in recent history.

INTERPRETATION

Throughout history men have misinterpreted God's word in an attempt to make it say what they want it to say. This has been done both deliberately and through simple error. But either way, to the extent these distortions are accepted or to the extent God's word is displaced by man's word, and because obedience is misdirected and led away from the truth, man suffers for it.

Much of what we read in Scripture is difficult to comprehend or may seem incredible because it doesn't conform to our experience. A virgin giving birth or the resurrection of a man dead for four days contradicts all our understanding as well as modern science. Our inclination is to reject the whole notion and to look for another explanation, one that agrees with what we see in the world around us. But the Bible doesn't let us do this; these and other miracles are attested to over and over again and cannot be dispensed with so easily. We cannot deny the miracles or any aspect of Scripture without also denying Biblical authority and stripping it of any validity whatsoever. In other words, the Bible must be taken as a whole in all its claims, or it must be set aside altogether.

But man—never satisfied with God's word—attempts, through interpretation, to introduce his own ideas while retaining an appearance of Scriptural authority. This process deceives the great majority of Christians who rely on pastors and seminary-educated theologians to tell them what the Bible says and means. They may believe they are obeying God but, in many cases, are actually being led astray by their teachers. These in turn may be sincere, thinking they are teaching truth but actually following the feelings of their own hearts or what others have taught them. This appears to be the case with many Bible school graduates who seem to have been taught strictly from a particular theological viewpoint—typically one that has arisen in the last century or so—and have little or no idea that other viewpoints (that may be very well supported from Scripture) even exist.

Liberal theologians have taken it upon themselves to question, distort, and redefine the plain statements in Scripture to the point of unrecognizability. They have, in effect, rewritten the Bible by imposing their ideas (what they would like it to say) in their interpretations. To the extent they have done this, and it has not been trivial, they have converted the inspired word of God into a human document. Without the pure word of God, ignorance reigns supreme and plunges many into total darkness. A form of Christianity remains, but its content is highly divergent from God's truth (see 2 Tim. 3:5). The work of these liberal theologians has cast a pall of darkness over much of the civilized world.

Conservative churches and theologians have not bought into much of this, but many of them are actually still deficient in that they attempt to conserve errors and distortions introduced by their predecessors. This is usually done with the best of intentions in an effort to preserve what is sincerely believed to be the truth but nevertheless is heresy. The problem we face today is multigenerational in duration. As a consequence, error that crept into the church a century or more ago is now accepted dogma and anyone who attempts to contradict it is branded a heretic. Churches and seminaries typically pay lip service to a policy of continual reformation process. They claim to be open to criticism and ready to give different viewpoints a fair hearing; but because this is an arduous, ongoing task and because they are so sure they already know everything they need to know, it soon goes by the boards and doctrinal rigor mortis sets in.

We read in 1 Corinthians 11:19, "For there must be also heresies among you, that they which are approved may be made manifest among you." God tells us here that we are still learning and that doctrines that may appear heretical should not be discarded without being given a fair trial. Because we are not gods, the way we approach the truth is not without error and stumbling along the way. When each school of theology puts on blinders and refuses to give sufficient consideration to the others, progress is impeded or comes to a halt. Sadly, this is very much the case today.

The absolute authority and straightforward interpretation of the Bible as the infallible word of the Creator God are indispensable to the maintenance of faith on earth. History suggests that when this is left to clerics only (theologians, priests, pastors, bishops, etc.), truth trends toward compromise and degradation. Without a Biblically knowledgeable Christian population—where a majority of believers spend sufficient time in study to understand the teachings—false teachings arise, take root, and multiply, seemingly without limit. It appears there are always enough gullible supporters available to populate and finance attractive yet unbiblical ideas. The history of Christianity in the twentieth century and presently in America demonstrates this tendency with great clarity.[13]

---

13 Winthrop S. Hudson, *Religion in America.* NY: Macmillan Publishing Co., 1992, 265 ff.

5

God's Plan

The Charter

THE creation of man is described in the first chapter of Genesis:

26 And God said, Let us make man in our image, after our likeness: and let them have dominion over the fish of the sea, and over the fowl of the air, and over the cattle, and over all the earth, and over every creeping thing that creepeth upon the earth.

27 So God created man in his own image, in the image of God created he him; male and female created he them.

28 And God blessed them, and God said unto them, Be fruitful, and multiply, and replenish the earth, and subdue it: and have dominion over the fish of the sea, and over the fowl of the air, and over every living thing that moveth upon the earth....

31 And God saw every thing that he had made, and, behold, it was very good. And the evening and the morning were the sixth day.

We see here that God made mankind, male and female, in His own image. Man was, of course, finite and limited—he could not be omnipotent, omniscient, or omnipresent as God is—but he was like God in many respects. He shared, to the extent a creature can, God's attributes of love, righteousness, and goodness. He, unlike the animals or any other creatures, was morally conscious. He was instructed as to right and wrong and given freedom of action to choose as he would. He was also given the responsibility to act as God's appointed head over the rest of the creation. He was to procreate (fill the earth with others of his own kind) and rule himself and all of creation in accordance with God's instructions.

Adam, with his wife Eve as his helper, was the absolute ruler over the entire earth. He was created to take charge of the whole earth. All its resources—the animals, plants, rivers, mountains, oceans, minerals, metals, and every asset it contained—were included. Adam's responsibility extended to future generations of mankind as well. He was the world's first king but, as we see in the next chapter, his rule was conditional. He was under God and subject to deposition by God if he deviated from God's conditions. He was directed to establish a world-order with God as the central authority and God's word the governing rule of law for this global community.

When God looked over all He had created, He said it was very good. This meant, because God is what He is, absolute perfection. There were no faults, nothing was missing or lacking. Development would follow, but everything needed was in place and ready. What was good was the creation itself as well as its purpose, the ultimate goal that Adam and Eve and their descendants were to fulfill. While we cannot comprehend all of God's purpose in creating this world and populating it with creatures capable of choosing obedience, we can surmise that His purpose included the establishment of what we would call today a Christian or Christ-centered world. To facilitate this, He placed into Adam's very being an innate desire to accomplish His instructions: "For it is God which worketh in you both to will and to do of His good pleasure" (Phil. 2:13). These God-embedded drives for dominion and procreation are the foremost of all human motivations.

But God did not create men as automatons that would do His will without thought or volition. He gave His creatures the ability to choose, to voluntarily obey or disobey Him. He then set up a test environment that would determine whether His creatures would obey Him or instead follow the model of Satan, Adam and Eve's predecessor in rebellion.

THE TEST

In the second chapter of Genesis, we see the test God prepared for Adam and Eve. They were given freedom of choice and God established a particular tree as the testing ground.

> 8 And the LORD God planted a garden eastward in Eden; and there he put the man whom he had formed....
>
> 15 And the LORD God took the man, and put him into the garden of Eden to dress it and to keep it.
>
> 16 And the LORD God commanded the man, saying, Of every tree of the garden thou mayest freely eat:
>
> 17 But of the tree of the knowledge of good and evil, thou shalt not eat of it: for in the day that thou eatest thereof thou shalt surely die.

God gave Adam and Eve a garden, perfect in every respect, a starter kit and a model for Adam to follow. As his family grew, he was to gradually enlarge it until, presumably many generations later, it would cover the whole earth.

The giving of the commandment regarding the forbidden fruit shows that man was under God and was to take dominion over the earth in accordance with God's rules and regulations. Any attempt to take dominion independently of God's Law-Word would be sin. The choice was quite simple: obedience would foster life and happiness; disobedience would bring separation and death. We know this because Scripture says so, but we can also surmise that it was the case simply because that was how God created man. Man was never meant, designed, or created to be able to live entirely on his own. He needed God's presence and God's directions in order to survive and be able to live life in the fullness God had provided for him. Death for disobedience then may not have been so much a punishment as it was a natural consequence.

The test was to see whether Adam and Eve would choose to remain under God's authority or—as Satan did before them—grasp for their own godhood. God required willing servants, not slavish robots; so God gave them a choice. Believe God or believe Satan.

FAILURE

In Genesis 3 we see the choice that was made and the beginning of the next stage of human history:

> 1 Now the serpent was more subtle than any beast of the field which the LORD God had made. And he said unto the woman, Yea, hath God said, Ye shall not eat of every tree of the garden?
>
> 2 And the woman said unto the serpent, We may eat of the fruit of the trees of the garden:
>
> 3 But of the fruit of the tree which is in the midst of the garden, God hath said, Ye shall not eat of it, neither shall ye touch it, lest ye die.
>
> 4 And the serpent said unto the woman, Ye shall not surely die:
>
> 5 For God doth know that in the day ye eat thereof, then your eyes shall be opened, and ye shall be as gods, knowing good and evil.
>
> 6 And when the woman saw that the tree was good for food, and that it was pleasant to the eyes, and a tree to be desired to make one wise, she took of the fruit thereof, and did eat, and gave also unto her husband with her; and he did eat.

Here we see their terrible decision. Our first parents decided to go it on their own, without God, and from that moment, all of history turned upside down. They chose to believe Satan and accept his advice rather than believe God. They desired to be "like God, knowing good and evil." That is to say, they wanted to decide for themselves concerning good and evil (or right and wrong). They wanted to fully direct their own lives without God's annoying commandments interfering with their personal preferences or chosen lifestyles.

Does this sound familiar? We hear it all the time and from virtually every source today. It seems everyone wants to decide his or her own lifestyle choices and most become indignant at any suggestion that they should not be able to do so. This is true even of many Christians today as well as non-believers. They believe they are Christians because they chose to be, but fail to recognize that God chose them long before they made their choice for Him (see Eph. 1:1–5, 11). They see themselves as self-determining entities able to shape their own destinies and in this respect stand level with God. These unbelievers (or misguided believers) fail to see that self-determination is an aspect of divinity. We are all God's creatures and as such are subject to His sovereign control of all things. Whatever freedom of action He has given us is still within His ultimate determination of everything that happens.[14]

A significant question regarding the Fall of mankind is *why*? Why did the decision of two people back at the beginning of history propagate through all the generations that followed, and why did it so permeate the character and personalities of the entire human race? The answer to this question is found in the penalty God imposed for disobedience. He said, "In the day that you eat of it, you shall surely die." But we know they did not die physically, at least not immediately. Some other sort of death took place at once. This death was spiritual; it involved an ethical distortion of their outlook, which was propagated to all succeeding generations. The image of God was still in man but it was distorted, not physically, but ethically. Man's outlook became self-centered rather than God-centered; obedience to God was replaced by an egocentric motivation. Since then, every new baby brought into the world has been born spiritually dead, out of contact with and spiritually separated from God. It is only in Christ that we see this condition reversed, with many being born again or "born of the Spirit" (see John 3:5–6; Eph. 2:1–6).

The ramifications of our first parents' decision stretch throughout all of history. Man, attempting the impossible—that is, finding his own way without God—is continually frustrated. Civilizations rise and fall, never realizing any kind of lasting unanimity, peace, or prosperity because these goals cannot be achieved apart from God's guidance and direction. Let's take note of three significant consequences that flow from this decision:

First, we see the basis of all sin: Man became self-centered instead of God-centered. He now has an inborn desire to make his own decisions and chart his own course. Each person seeks primarily to please

14 God's sovereignty is explicitly taught in Scripture. To deny it is to allow the whole fabric of Christianity to unravel. If just one thing were outside His control, God would no longer be God, prophecy would be uncertain, God could not answer prayer, and the laws of physics would give way to a universe based on chance where anything could happen." See Martin Luther, *The Bondage of the Will*, trans. J. I. Packer and O. R. Johnston. Grand Rapids, MI: Fleming H. Revell, division of Baker Publishing Group, 1959, 83–86.

himself and attempts to get as much as he can for himself. Success today is equated with wealth, the ability to lavish upon oneself more and more of the luxuries of life, the ability to control one's own destiny, and to do as one pleases whenever one pleases. These are the essential elements of deviant "god-likeness," the rationale Satan cited for disobedience to God. When a person is his own god, he becomes the all-important one; the well-being of others is diminished (or entirely discounted) and selfishness becomes central. This is not to say that unselfish deeds are never done. It's just that they are exceptions, deviations from the basic drive for selfish gain that lies in men's hearts. Where we see unselfish deeds on the part of a disobedient person, they are generally the consequence of custom or training; they are not inborn characteristics; they are foreign to his nature at birth (see Rom. 1:28–32; Eph. 2:1–6).

Second, the God-given dominion motivation is still operative but it is misdirected. Natural man, that is, man as he is born into this world, is still dominion-oriented; his predilection is to advance himself as much as possible, and, whenever necessary, at the expense of his neighbor. Dominion as practiced by sinful man has degraded to domination over everyone else for totally selfish purposes. We see this today in the drive toward a totalitarian, socialistic, one-world government—a government that utterly denies God and attempts to set itself up as "god" over the entire world's population. Ungodly dominion is particularly directed against God and God's people. The natural man desires to suppress his knowledge of God and works against any and all who proclaim God's word or try to make Him known.

Third, man could no longer do God's work. He disqualified himself by denying God's sovereignty. Another Adam and a whole new humanity—a new family line after the "second Adam"—would be needed to perform that function. More on this subject will follow.

A question that often arises at this point is why did God permit this disaster to take place? Why didn't He make Adam and Eve so that they would be able to resist Satan and choose correctly? Very frankly, there is no answer, but before asking any question that begins with "why did God…," two things must be taken into consideration.

First, we must recognize that God's knowledge exceeds our own by a huge (actually infinite) amount. We cannot begin to comprehend more than the very tiniest fraction of what He knows, and, truthfully, we are limited to what He chooses to reveal to us. What He does not reveal remains unknown, at least for now. "The secret things belong unto the LORD our God: but those things which are revealed belong unto us and to our children forever, that we may do all the words of this law" (Deut. 29:29).

Second, our questioning God may stem from wanting to exercise a moral judgment of His action. We need to consider that there is no basis for any such judgment other than God Himself. There is no standard that can be placed above God against which His actions may be criticized. Moral judgments must be rooted in some foundational, universal, invariant morality in order to avoid being arbitrary. The ultimate standard of morality is God's eternal character itself, for He is absolutely perfect in His very being. Therefore all of His actions are good because they flow from His holy character. When we challenge God, we erect an independent standard and abandon Him as the standard of truth and righteousness. This causes us to fall into the very sin of Adam and Eve, for Satan's temptation to them was: "ye shall be as gods, knowing [determining] good and evil" (Gen. 3:5b).

The Fall of man, of course, changed everything, as we read in Genesis chapter 3:

> 14 And the LORD God said unto the serpent, Because thou hast done this, thou art cursed above all cattle, and above every beast of the field; upon thy belly shalt thou go, and dust shalt thou eat all the days of thy life:
>
> 15 And I will put enmity between thee and the woman, and between thy seed and her seed; it shall bruise thy head, and thou shalt bruise his heel.
>
> 16 Unto the woman he said, I will greatly multiply thy sorrow and thy conception; in sorrow thou shalt bring forth children; and thy desire shall be to thy husband, and he shall rule over thee.
>
> 17 And unto Adam he said, Because thou hast hearkened unto the voice of thy wife, and hast eaten of the tree, of which I commanded thee, saying, Thou shalt not eat of it: cursed is the ground for thy sake; in sorrow shalt thou eat of it all the days of thy life;

18 Thorns also and thistles shall it bring forth to thee; and thou shalt eat the herb of the field;

19 In the sweat of thy face shalt thou eat bread, till thou return unto the ground; for out of it wast thou taken: for dust thou art, and unto dust shalt thou return.

Adam and Eve were evicted from the garden where they had enjoyed the blessings and provision of God in every way. Now Adam would have to work much harder for his sustenance and Eve would experience much pain in childbirth. But God also displayed mercy at this time; He told them something about the future that their offspring would experience and also offered them a cause for hope. There was to be a struggle between the seed of the woman and the seed of the serpent; a struggle in which the woman's seed would triumph. This text is known as the *proto-evangellium*, the first statement of the Gospel in Scripture. We learn later in Scripture that Christ is the promised seed of the woman (see Gal. 3:16,19).

God knew Adam and Eve would fall into temptation and disobey him. So He had already set in place a plan for the redemption of the human race. The Son of God, part of the Godhead, would take on the human nature—become a man—and die as a substitute for all who would believe in Him.

In addition, we learn that those who believe in the Son of God are made "a new creation," a new kind of people in whom "old things have passed away" and "all things are become new" (see 2 Cor. 5:17). This new humanity is also the seed of the woman, while all those who do not believe constitute the seed of the devil (see 1 Cor. 12:27; Gal. 3:29, 6:15; 1 Pet. 2:5; John 8:42–45;. 1 Jo. 3:10).

It is these two groups of mankind—those "in Christ" and those "in Adam," believers and unbelievers—who have been in perpetual opposition and conflict with each other throughout all of history. God, by placing enmity between the two seeds (see Gen. 3:15), insured that this strife would be maintained. Now this may sound as if it is somewhat out of character for God. After all, God commands us to love one another and the Apostle John tells us that "God is love" (see 1 John 4:8). So why should a loving God set these two groups of men against each other? The answer to this paradox will become evident as we look at the next stage of God's plan, the Great Commission.

6

THE GREAT COMMISSION

CHRIST's last word to His disciples is found in Matthew 28:

18 And Jesus came and spake unto them, saying, All power is given unto me in heaven and in earth.

19 Go ye therefore, and teach all nations, baptizing them in the name of the Father, and of the Son, and of the Holy Ghost:

20 Teaching them to observe all things whatsoever I have commanded you: and, lo, I am with you always, even unto the end of the world. Amen.

This is, in effect, a restatement of the Dominion Mandate of Genesis 1. He directs His disciples, and by implication all Christians, to "teach all nations" to "observe all things whatsoever I have commanded you." Christ is telling His people, all those who are in Christ, that "all power" has been given to Him (i.e., Satan's power has been broken) and they should now go out into the world and complete the work the first Adam failed to do. Christ at this point declares Himself the rightful ruler of all the nations of the earth; hence the nations are required to obey Him in all things. This statement of Christ's authority should not be restricted to some nebulous, spiritual sense. The disciples were in the world, we are in the world, and it is the nations of the world that are in view here. Christ's authority is over all nations, which covers all the people in the world. It is not just Christians that are required to submit to Christ and obey His commandments. While we recognize that a large segment of the population deny

Christ and refuse to submit to His rule, this does not alter the fact of His reign over them. It is significant that Christ is called the second Adam: "And so it is written, The first man Adam was made a living soul; the last Adam was made a quickening spirit" (1 Cor. 15:45).

The first Adam forsook the responsibilities God placed on him. He was to multiply and fill the earth and take dominion over it in God's name and in accordance with God's law. In view was a world that honored God in every respect, a world that obeyed God's commandments without compromise or deviation of any kind—a world without sin. Adam failed miserably, but God's plan was not frustrated: He knew Adam would be unsuccessful and together with the Son and the Holy Spirit had already prepared a way to realize His original intent for the earth and its people. Christ, as the second Adam, would do what the first Adam failed to do. First was the Incarnation in which the Son of God took on the human nature. As a man, though without sin, He was able to go to the cross and take upon Himself the penalty for all sin.

This done, the Holy Spirit was sent to apply the forgiveness of sin to all of God's elect (see John 3:5–6; 1 Cor. 6:11). The Holy Spirit opened their eyes; they believed God and were saved from death unto eternal life. But more was required. The world was still largely sinful and did not begin to approach the ideal God had established at creation. This new humanity that was brought into existence, Christ's brothers and sisters, the seed of the woman, were given their marching orders in the Great Commission. There was a whole sinful world that needed cleaning up. They were told to go out, to preach, to baptize, and to convert the world to Christ. In short, to do what the first Adam failed to do: to bring into existence a Christian world, a world that hallows God's name and does His will.

Notice here that while the original mandate to take dominion over the earth was given to an individual (Adam), by implication it also included all his offspring. The task was far too great to be accomplished by a single person; it would have required many generations to fulfill. So, too, the completion of the task of the second Adam, Jesus Christ, has been assigned to all those who are "in Christ," all who have been born again and are His spiritual offspring. This is the assignment that God has placed before every Christian in the world today and in the generations to follow. As Christians, we have a cosmic purpose, one that transcends the petty issues we deal with every day. It should stand above every other goal or vision we hold as Christians. A desire to obey the God who has done so much for us should burn in our hearts throughout our lives.

God's view differs from ours. He saw the whole human race in the person of Adam and now sees all believers in Christ. This viewpoint can be seen in what God said about Melchizedek (see Heb. 7:1–10). He said that Levi gave tithes to Melchizedek when it was Abraham, Levi's ancestor that did so hundreds of years earlier. God saw "in Abraham" all his descendants throughout time. They are referred to as if they were a part of his person. Likewise He sees "in Christ" every sinner in all of history that is born again and repents. There is an organic connection within the body of Christ: Christ is the head and all true believers form the body (see Eph. 4:14–16). It should not seem so strange then that some of the work ascribed to Christ should be completed by the members of His body rather than by Christ personally.

When Christ on the cross uttered His last words, "It is finished," He was not saying that there was nothing left to be done. Jesus' personal work was completed but there was still a world to be brought into submission to Him.

THE ANTITHESIS

The enmity that God placed between the seed of the woman and the seed of the serpent was intended, *first*: to insure that the two groups would remain distinct from each other (no middle-of-the-road compromises with evil), and, *second*: to insure that the good seed would continue to fight against the evil, that it would not give up and allow godlessness to take dominion in its place.

But this is just what America's Christians have done. Too many of them have withdrawn from public affairs and have not retained the cultural control they exercised in the nineteenth century and before. They have stood back, done nothing, and allowed humanism free-reign. Before this evil trend can be corrected, it needs to be understood. We, as God's people, need to see where we have gone wrong and make whatever corrections are necessary, however painful they may be. Only then can the current trend be halted and eventually reversed.

These two seeds—having existed and struggled against each other throughout all of history—can be thought of as consistent Christians and consistent humanists. The qualification of consistency is necessary because of all the philosophical spillover that exists in practice. Christian believers recognize this in the doctrine of sanctification, a lifelong process of separation from the world. It involves shedding the "Old Man," old ideas that predate the conversion experience and are inconsistent with the new faith. Likewise, humanists never lose all the Biblical principles that permeate the Western worldview in which they are brought up.

The very first son born to Adam and Eve murdered the second son and so this struggle has continued for all the generations that followed. Good and evil, God's way and man's (or Satan's) way are always and everywhere in opposition and have at their root this basic, fundamental difference in worldviews. Both are still imbued with the drive to take dominion: One attempts to do so under God and in obedience to Him, the other in rebellion against God and His law.

Although many attempts have been made to do so throughout history, no bridge can be built to join these two disparate forces together. There is no conciliation or compromise that can be effected. God created this antithesis when He put the enmity in place; it is rooted in the very fiber of our beings and cannot be eradicated. Christ alluded to the antithesis when He said in Matthew 10:

> 34 Think not that I am come to send peace on earth: I came not to send peace, but a sword.
>
> 35 For I am come to set a man at variance against his father, and the daughter against her mother, and the daughter in law against her mother in law.
>
> 36 And a man's foes shall be they of his own household.

Christ's coming introduces discord so sharp as to divide families in two and peace gives way to the sword.

The line of demarcation between the two groups is not clearly drawn today. There are many middle-of-the-road types that are neither fish nor fowl: Christians that cling to humanistic ideas and humanists that sometimes appear more "Christian" than many Christians. These individuals muddy the water and tend to hide the fact of the antithesis.

In actuality, there are two kinds of humanity in the world. They are physically identical but very different spiritually and hold to opposite ideas as to what constitutes reality. Even though the distinctions are very blurred today, these two mutually exclusive worldviews will always continue to struggle for dominance. Eventually one or the other will prevail; one day the world will either be dominated by Christianity or entirely devoid of Christianity. The answer to Christ's question, "Nevertheless when the Son of man cometh, shall He find faith on the earth?" (see Luke 18:8), lies in the balance.

WHEAT AND TARES

Matthew 13:

> 24 Another parable put He forth unto them, saying, The kingdom of heaven is likened unto a man which sowed good seed in his field:
>
> 25 But while men slept, his enemy came and sowed tares among the wheat, and went his way.
>
> 26 But when the blade was sprung up, and brought forth fruit, then appeared the tares also.
>
> 27 So the servants of the householder came and said unto him, Sir, didst not thou sow good seed in thy field? from whence then hath it tares?
>
> 28 He said unto them, An enemy hath done this. The servants said unto him, Wilt thou then that we go and gather them up?
>
> 29 But he said, Nay; lest while ye gather up the tares, ye root up also the wheat with them.
>
> 30 Let both grow together until the harvest: and in the time of harvest I will say to the reapers, Gather ye together first the tares, and bind them in bundles to burn them: but gather the wheat into my barn.

In this parable, Christ reflects back to God's pronouncement of enmity between the two seeds at the Fall. It depicts the history and end result of the protracted struggle between the opposing worldviews of Christianity and humanism.

Christ sowed the good seed—His people, all who believe in Him—into the world. Likewise, the enemy (the devil) sowed the bad seed: his people, the unbelievers, all those who choose not to have God to rule over them. This was his attempt to frustrate God's plan to raise only a good crop: a world populated with faithful, obedient men and women. But God's plans are never frustrated, so as Christ says in the parable, the world will eventually end up with only the good remaining. All who offend and them which do iniquity shall be cast into a furnace of fire (see verses 41, 42). Notice here, contrary to what so many of today's theologians tell us, it is the evil that are removed, not the good that are raptured away.

But in the meantime, before the end of the world, the wheat and the tares live side by side and of necessity must compete for growing space. If the wheat did not compete, the tares would soon overwhelm it and by the end of the growing season nothing would be left but weeds. Likewise when Christians (the good seed) fail to resist the encroachment of unbelievers, they are crowded out, their numbers diminish, and intolerance followed by persecution ensues.

The householder in the parable told his servants not to pluck up the tares until the wheat became sufficiently mature to withstand the turmoil involved. The young plants could not be easily distinguished from one another and good wheat could be lost in the process. Likewise, today Christians and unbelievers are not so different as to be easily distinguishable from one another. But as the two groups each become more consistent to their relative faiths, the differences become more and more pronounced, the antithesis becomes better defined, and the dissimilarities become more obvious. It may be that one of God's purposes in history is to strengthen this antithesis so that the distinction between good and evil becomes more clearly defined and the two groups become more aware of both where they stand and the consequences of their choices.

The Christian faith prospers and grows—both in terms of numbers and in terms of depth of commitment—in an environment that is supportive of the faith. It languishes and shrinks in an environment such as we see today in America. Christian youth need to be nurtured in a Christian culture. Their faith is undermined when they are required to attend schools where teachers may not even mention God's name, where in all their classes the teachings are as if God is irrelevant or nonexistent.

As a consequence of this kind of exposure to atheism, both in schools and in the entertainment media, large numbers of young people brought up in Bible-believing, church-going Christian homes lose their faith.[15]

Sadly, it is those students who do best, who excel in their schoolwork and then go on to institutions of higher learning (where the atheistic propaganda is even more intense), that are most affected. This has led to the current situation where the educated class, the intellectuals in this country, are preponderantly non-Christian. But these are our leaders, congressmen, senators, judges; they shape the laws we live under, laws such as abortion rights, hate speech legislation, and toleration of pornography and homosexuality. It is a vicious circle: a little unbelief produces more and more unbelief with each generation, and the atheistic tares force out the wheat and take over the ground.

SALT AND LIGHT

Matthew 5:

> 13 Ye are the salt of the earth: but if the salt have lost his savour, wherewith shall it be salted? It is thenceforth good for nothing, but to be cast out, and to be trodden under foot of men.
>
> 14 Ye are the light of the world. A city that is set on an hill cannot be hid.

When Christ told all who believe in Him that they were the salt of the earth and the light of the world, He didn't say "you are *a salting factor*" or "you are *a* light." Jesus warns that it is up to *us* to keep our *saltiness*. Just as salt preserves meat from spoiling, Christians are required to keep the world from corrupting.

Without the restraint of God's laws operating on the public at large, evil spreads and permeates society; the wicked rise in power and promote their wicked cronies to positions of authority. They take control of schools and other institutions and lead the city or nation farther and farther from God's word. Evil grows like a cancer and there is nothing

---

15 See "Most Twentysomethings Put Christianity on the Shelf Following Spiritually Active Teen Years," Barna Group Study, September 11, 2006: http://www.barna.org/ teens-next-gen-articles/147-most-twentysomethings-put-christianity-on-the-shelf-following-spiritually-active-teen-years.

to hold it back other than Christ's salt—His people. As the influence of Christianity recedes, the world grows more and more corrupt and darkness predominates in society.

As Christian influence gains ground, evil diminishes and righteousness can begin to grow and replace it. This is the task each Christian is called to by his Lord. It's not just to go out and preach the word to unbelievers. Yes, that is also needed, but to be the salt of the earth is much more—it is to get involved in politics, in government, in law, in education, in entertainment, and in every field or institution that influences the culture. No one can get involved in *every* area, but each of us has a degree of influence *somewhere*. Christ calls us to exert that influence to further the advance of His kingdom in this world. When the seemingly miniscule efforts of each individual are multiplied by the numbers in a Christian population, the total effect can be enormous. Mountains can be moved; the world can be changed.

Christ said that He is the light of the world (see John 8:12). The primary, fundamental, and only truth in the world is Christ Himself and without His word, there is only darkness, blindness, and ignorance. Christian, do you believe this? Was the Lord exaggerating when He uttered these words, or did He mean exactly what He said? Is He or is He not the source of all knowledge?[16]

Do you think that science has knowledge that is independent of Christ and that can remain in His absence? Most Christians today would probably say yes, the basic sciences represent an objective factual knowledge that is shared by both unbelievers and believers and therefore seems independent of Christ. But how is this possible? How can one arrive at truth when one begins with utterly preposterous first principles such as chance, which governs evolution and spontaneous generation? Over and over again, whenever science has deviated from Scripture, it has been found to be false and Scripture true. Christians—particularly those of you in the sciences—need to stop taking a back seat and allowing atheists to take the lead. They have no solid ground to stand on and you need to keep pointing this out.

---

16 Cornelius Van Til, *An Introduction to Systematic Theology.* Philippsburg, New Jersey: Presbyterian and Reformed Publishing Co., 1974, 21–30.

A further problem with denying the light of Christ is what happens to people's thinking when they attempt to believe something that deep down they know is wrong. James tells us that "a double minded man is unstable in all his ways" (see James 1:8). When someone allows confused thinking to exist in one area of thought, it affects all his thinking and he becomes "unstable in all his ways." Most of today's scientists, although deep down within they know that God exists (see Rom. 1:19–20), have accepted the theory of evolution and several other non-Biblical and illogical theories; consequently they have opened the door to double-mindedness. Because of this, and because they have ignored God's word, prevailing, modern, secular scientists are deviating from truth today in fields such as biology, economics, astronomy, and even basic physics.[17]

As the world moves away from God and God's word, knowledge will diminish rather than increase. As we see in these fields, this process has already begun. It is only the presence of true faith on earth that retards the rate of deterioration and keeps alive the level of civilization that we still enjoy.

The responsibility God has placed on Christians is extremely broad. It isn't limited to "spiritual" matters but includes all of life. We read in 2 Corinthians 10:3–5:

> 3 For though we walk in the flesh, we do not war after the flesh:
>
> 4 (For the weapons of our warfare are not carnal, but mighty through God to the pulling down of strong holds;)
>
> 5 Casting down imaginations, and every high thing that exalteth itself against the knowledge of God, and bringing into captivity every thought to the obedience of Christ.

Here we see that though Paul discourages using the sword to impose a Christian world-order (cp. Matt. 26:52), he urges Christians to recognize that we are, nevertheless, at war. But we are engaged in a war of ideas. The fallen world has its strongholds in its own vain philosophies, moral constructs, economic theories, political proposals, and so forth. But Christians must employ sound reasoning from Scripture to expose, defeat,

---

17 Magnus Verbrugge, M.D., *Alive: An Inquiry into the Origin and Meaning of Life.* Vallecito, CA: Ross House Books, 1984. For more information, see the following websites: www.icr.org; www.mises.org; www.commonsensescience.org.

and replace those philosophies in the marketplace of ideas. As Paul says elsewhere, we must "have no fellowship with the unfruitful works of darkness, but rather reprove them" (Eph. 5:11). That is, we must not share in the unworkable policies of fallen man, which are ultimately the works of sin and darkness. Instead, we must challenge unbelief and topple its vainglorious pronouncements by properly reasoning from the inspired, inerrant, revealed word of God. God's word is the ultimate, foundational truth. And God has called us to be "the light of the world" (Matt. 5:14), the whole world.

When Christ told Pilate that His kingdom was not *of* this world, He didn't say it was not *in* this world or that it should not have any effect in the world. He taught His disciples to pray "Thy kingdom come. Thy will be done in earth as it is in heaven" (see Matt. 6:9–13). This should not be limited to one's own life and that of his family and friends. It is nothing less than a prayer for the conversion of the world, for the world to recognize Christ as King of kings and Lord of lords. But how many Christians today say the words of this prayer week in and week out without a thought as to what it really means?

To be effective as salt and light, Christians must be knowledgeable of the content of God's word as it applies to life on earth, and this requires that they must also be aware of what is going on in the world. They cannot apply a word they misunderstand nor can they employ it to solve problems they are not aware of or do not understand properly.

Christians are the body of Christ, the manifestation of Christ's humanity on earth, and are called, as Adam was, to take dominion and to oversee the whole earth. They have been given the task of the first Adam and the power of the indwelling Holy Spirit to accomplish it. Sadly, we have not been faithful to this Great Commission of Christ. We have formulated all sorts of excuses for our failure and need to beg His forgiveness and get back on track.

DUTY

Today's church has to a great extent trivialized the sense of Christ's words by reducing them to a directive to merely preach the Gospel to all nations. But this is not what the words say; we are instructed to teach the nations and bring them into obedience to Christ's commandments.

This involves much more than just preaching. Major cultural changes, requiring a long-term commitment to education, leadership, training in godly living, and much more, are in view here. At the end of World War II, General Douglas MacArthur called for 10,000 missionaries to help rebuild, reorient, and bring Christian civilization to Japan. While this number was probably insufficient to the task, he had the right idea. It was "Christian civilization" that was needed there and just what Christ commanded 2,000 years earlier. The U.S. did not send anywhere near 10,000 missionaries and Japan remains mostly a heathen nation today.

The Great Commission is nothing less than an edict for the restoration of the world. And this is the sense in which the church understood it up to a century or two ago. We need to shake off our foolishness and see that the Great Commission is not merely a call to preach the Gospel and get as many people saved as possible. It is a command to convert all the nations of the world to Christ and to teach them obedience.

This trivializing of the Great Commission is undergirded by a highly spiritualized view of Scripture, a view that insists on seeing spiritual meanings behind simple, common, everyday statements. The physical world is viewed as a temporary platform, solely a training and testing ground in which we make decisions that determine our final destiny. The world and references to life here are constantly pushed into the background as if the only things that happen here of any significance are spiritual in nature. Proponents of this view are quite ready to let the world become more and more corrupt and do nothing to change it. But the great preponderance of Scripture deals with life in this world; in fact, very little is said about heaven and what life in heaven will be like.

God has a purpose for this world and has given us instructions regarding our part in that purpose. We have been given very specific assignments that relate to our life here. We must not distort His word to make excuses for our failure to carry out His commandments. We are to be the salt that preserves and the light that instructs the nations of the world. It is our failure to perform these functions that has led to the pitiful present condition of the world.

This task is one that involves all Christians, not just those already in the "Lord's work" such as ministers, evangelists, and missionaries. It entails a complete restructuring of the present humanistic society along Biblical lines. Education, entertainment, law, politics, business, medicine—all of man's endeavors—need major overhauling before a truly godly society can be built. The work of the clergy is not to do all this themselves, but to teach and prepare the saints to also do this work (Eph. 4:11-13).

The primary thrust of preaching should be in support of the membership of the church, to help them come to a better understanding of the responsibilities that fall on God's people as a consequence of this Great Commission Christ has placed on them. They are ever in need of Scriptural guidance to show them how to select objectives, establish goals, and interact with the world in carrying out what should be a lifelong purpose for them.

The work being done (or that should be done) by all Christians requires and deserves a great deal more effort and financial support than does the preaching of the Gospel. Scripture reflects this in the law structure God gave the nation of Israel where the tithe was given to the Levites, who provided a wide range of services for the community, including education, medical care, courts of adjudication, leadership, and many other services. This was where the bulk of the tithe went; only a tithe of the tithe went to support the Priests. In the America of the nineteenth century, large numbers of tithe agencies provided most of these functions.[18] Today, however, various levels of civil government now provide virtually all these services, and people, even Christians, look to the state to provide for them. As Christians withdrew from these areas, the state moved in, and what were once religious functions have become secular and Godless.

The loss of focus on the Great Commission as a comprehensive task for all Christians and its degeneration into only a call to preach has robbed God's people of the primary purpose God gave them. In this scenario, the pulpits and the mission field are considered the real work. All church members are required to do is turn over the tithe to the church, live moral lives, and set a good example to those around them. There is no need to work for godliness in education, entertainment, or government. As a

---

18 E. A. Powell and R. J. Rushdoony, *Tithing and Dominion.* Vallecito, CA: Ross House Books, 1979, 26; Richard Henry Dana Jr., *Two Years Before the Mast.* New York: Harper & Brothers, 1842, 477–478; Alexis de Tocqueville, *Democracy in America.* New York: Edward Walker, 1847, 8, 208, 209.

consequence, Christians have withdrawn from the world to such an extent that they are no longer involved in significant culture-changing activities. They are like salt that has lost its savor (Matt. 5:13). The moral degeneration of America in the past several decades can be directly attributed to this abandonment by Christians of the responsibility Christ placed on them. He instructed us to be salt and light and we have reduced this to light only—and a dim one at that.

The greater culpability in this lies at the feet of those ministers and theologians who, having paid too much attention to newspapers, have lost faith in ever achieving what Christ commanded us to do. Their subsequent revision of Scripture teaching has moved much of the church from the hope of victory to despair. The general belief is that the forces of evil are just too strong for us and victory is only possible with the Lord's return. This appears to have become a self-fulfilling prophecy, and, as a consequence, a large part of the church now considers itself resigned to a struggle for existence in a world given over to the devil.

The modern church's limited view of the Great Commission has been a major factor leading to the decline in Christian influence around the world. It is part and parcel of a generally accepted pessimistic attitude on the part of Christian leadership. It is, effectively, a thinly veiled excuse for failure. As the world has become worse due to the lack of Christian involvement, much of Christian leadership responded with a reinterpretation of Scripture, one that says we're doing all we have been instructed to do. In other words, when we don't like the results, just redefine our objectives to bring them into line with the results. This is a fairly common technique used to obfuscate failure and incompetence, but it is not one that true Christians should employ.

These misleading teachings must be corrected before the current slide into moral and religious depravity can begin to be reversed. God's people need to have their great purpose for living restored. They need to both, 1) gain an understanding of what their responsibilities are, and 2) regain the hope of eventual victory—before they can begin to take the measures required to halt the current trend into oblivion. This process would be expedited if the pulpits would take the lead and begin to teach Biblically. But, realistically, it will probably not come about until the situation becomes so grave that those in the pews rebel and demand new leadership.

The future is bright with hope, the only question being *how and when*. How long will it take for Christians to get back on track, straighten themselves out, and then fix the mess this world has become? Actually, there is good cause for optimism rather than pessimism. Immediately upon giving the Great Commission, Christ promised: "lo, I am with you always, even unto the end of the world. Amen" (see Matt. 28:20). Christ is still seated at the right hand of God, but He is "with us" in the person of the Holy Spirit.

Too many Christians have spent too much time looking at world events and too little time listening to God's promises. They have succumbed to Satan's lies expressed by men such as Charles Darwin and other minions he employs to discourage God's people and dissuade them from their Christ-given responsibilities. We need to hold fast to His promise that He will be with us to the end of the world, and not lose heart. Don't let Satan confuse us with deceptively smooth words as he did Eve and then Adam. He is most happy to see Christians in the state of confusion and misdirection that pervades them today. This sorry state of affairs is not what Christ had in mind when He told us to disciple the nations and said He would always be with us, even to the end of the world.

7

GOD'S LAW

THROUGHOUT history God has demonstrated great patience with His creatures. When Adam and Eve sinned there were no faithful left on earth; but God later used Seth's line to restore faith (Gen. 4:26). Subsequently, except for Noah, that faith died out and God sent a flood to destroy the wickedness that had permeated mankind (Gen. 6:1–8). Faith on earth was reduced to eight persons that survived the flood. We are not told how long that faith persisted but by the time of the Tower of Babel it appears to have been gone. God then chose one man, Abram, whom He renamed Abraham (father of a multitude) and from him built a nation, a people that would carry the faith for the next two thousand years. He chose Moses, whom He had live as an Egyptian prince for forty years, a shepherd in the desert another forty years, and finally as the leader of Israel the final forty years of his life. Through Moses God provided a law system that would assure that the faith would be propagated. That law system was far and away the greatest and wisest ever seen by man. We read in Deuteronomy 4:

> 5 Behold, I have taught you statutes and judgments, even as the LORD my God commanded me, that ye should do so in the land whither ye go to possess it.
>
> 6 Keep therefore and do them; for this is your wisdom and your understanding in the sight of the nations, which shall

hear all these statutes, and say, Surely this great nation is a wise and understanding people.

7 For what nation is there so great, who hath God so nigh unto them, as the LORD our God is in all things that we call upon him for?

8 And what nation is there so great, that hath statutes and judgments so righteous as all this law, which I set before you this day?

God tells us here that this law was wisdom, understanding, and righteousness, that it would make the nation great if it were obeyed. It was exactly what was needed to establish a God-honoring and God-fearing culture. Israel was to be a seed that would expand and eventually cover the earth. Had Israel been faithful, the entire world would eventually have come under the umbrella of this law and would have enjoyed the many blessings to be derived therefrom. The Israelites though, were frequently a disappointment in that they repeatedly fell away from the path of obedience. But because they often did repent and return to God, embers of the faith were kept burning until the Son came.

Too many Christians today, through a reinterpretation of Scripture, have set aside this law, declaring it to have been countermanded by God in the New Testament. In so doing, they have effectively replaced God's Law with their own laws based on man's word rather than God's word. The consequences that flow from this unfortunate and sinful direction are manifold and serious. The wisdom, understanding, and righteousness of God's law they have sacrificed has left them, as peoples and nations, largely rudderless and struggling continuously for meaning and direction.

Even worse, to reject God's law is to reject God. Whether done outright or through a convenient reinterpretation of Scripture, it represents a denial of the Christian faith and threatens to deprive us of our only legitimate standard. It is every Christian's responsibility to study Scripture and discover what God Himself says about His law—not what revisionist theologians have to say.

God's law means a great deal to God. As R. J. Rushdoony put it:

Lawless Christianity is a contradiction in terms: it is anti-Christian. The purpose of grace is not to set aside the law but to fulfill the law and to enable man to keep the law. If the law was so serious in the sight of God that it would require the death of Jesus Christ, the only-begotten Son of God, to make atonement for man's sin, it seems strange for God then to proceed to abandon the law! The goal of the law is not lawlessness, nor the purpose of grace a lawless contempt of the giver of grace.[19]

The church has historically understood God's Old Testament Law as being comprised of three kinds of law. *First*, the *ritual* law, including the extreme cost of sin in terms of blood sacrifices, helped Israel to recognize the utter sinfulness of man and his need of a Savior. Virtually all Christians agree these were fulfilled in the work of Christ on the cross (Hebrews 7–10). *Second*, the great majority of Christians have maintained the centrality of the *Moral Law*—the Ten Commandments in particular, and the Two Great Commandments, a restatement by Jesus in the New Testament. *Third*, disagreement comes over the *judicial law*, specific laws with civil penalties. Many Christians have maintained that these laws ended with the Old Testament, except for the lasting general equity principles they illustrate, while others maintain they are still valid today.

Here Rushdoony gives us an answer. Leaving "general equity" vague and undefined opens doors for humanistic statism to affect the civil and judicial laws of Christian civilization. Is "general equity" what God says or what men say? It is clear that God means His Law-Word to be the same for all time (Matt. 24:35), which would indicate that the general equity, or applied principles, of the moral law given in the Old Testament, must be applicable and binding today, including in the civil realm.

Rushdoony explains that our civil, judicial, and criminal law must derive from moral principles: "That which is a rule of life for man is also a rule of life for his courts, civil governments, and institutions." Clearly godliness in the civil realm must derive from God's Moral law, centered on the Ten Commandments and the Two Commandments of Christ. Dr. Rushdoony takes the Mosaic judicial laws such as restitution plus a percentage for theft as a case law precedent from the moral law given as "You shall not steal." It makes no sense to have a moral law unless the

---

19 R. J. Rushdoony, *The Institutes of Biblical Law.* Nutley, NJ: Craig Press, 1973, 4.

judicial law reflects and enforces it, thus protecting justice according to God's command (Micah 6:8). The case law provides specific examples of the principles to be applied.[20]

The major portion of God's law is given in the form of case law, not statutory law. The Bible does not attempt to identify every kind of specific instance to which the law applies. Rather, we are expected to discern from cases given in the Bible what the underlying principles involved are and then apply those to each present case in question. One example of this is found in Deuteronomy 22:8: "When thou buildest a new house, then thou shalt make a battlement for thy roof, that thou bring not blood upon thine house, if any man fall from thence." The principle here is that we are responsible for the lives and well-being of our neighbors and must not leave an open hazard that could endanger them. Today we would say that one must have, for example, a fence or other barrier to prevent small children from falling into a swimming pool. But it isn't just about fences; it is unlawful to drive a vehicle with faulty brakes for the same reason. Today we don't install fences around our roofs because the roof is not used as a living space as it was in Moses' day, and, as a consequence, since there is no danger of neighbors falling off our roofs, we are not in violation of God's law. Please notice, this does not constitute a change in the law; the law was always one of principle.

THE NEED FOR LAW

God, as Creator and the ultimate standard of morality, is also man's rightful lawgiver. He created us and therefore has every right to subject us to whatever laws He deems fit. Christ tells us in Matthew 4:4: "It is written, Man shall not live by bread alone, but by every word that proceedeth out of the mouth of God."

This statement from our Lord tells us that it is not only food that is essential to life. Without food, man starves and dies; without God's Law-Word, man is also susceptible to death but in a different form. He either becomes directionless or pursues goals that are not conducive to a healthy and meaningful way of life. His sin nature always leads him away

---

20 Rousas John Rushdoony, *Institutes of Biblical Law.* The Presbyterian and Reformed Publishing company, 1973, 550-551.

from life and toward death. God's word, His *every* word—which includes His law—is an indispensable requirement, not just for eternal life but for life in this world.

Indeed, God's law has always been with His creatures. In the Garden of Eden, He established a law with Adam and Eve that tested them to see whether or not they would obey. They were forbidden to eat of the tree in the midst of the garden. Their first children, Cain and Abel, were subject to laws governing their offerings and with respect to murder. Law was in effect when God sent the flood to destroy all but eight people because He "saw that the wickedness of man was great in the earth, and that every imagination of the thoughts of his heart was only evil continually" (see Gen. 6:5). Noah was told, "Whoso sheddeth man's blood, by man shall his blood be shed: for in the image of God made he man" (see Gen. 9:6). Man has never been without God's law.

When God liberated His chosen people from slavery in Egypt and gave them their own land to live in, He gave them a detailed law code that showed them how to order their lives in the new land. But this was not entirely new information; law existed prior to Moses. Law had always existed, even prior to the Fall. However, after the Fall there was a much greater need for more strict rules to counter man's desire to be his own god, to decide for himself what is right and what is wrong.

Man—especially fallen man—cannot live without law. God didn't create us to live independently of Him and His law. Even Adam before the Fall was not left to himself. God instructed him as they walked together in the cool of the day (see Gen. 1:28–30, 2:16–17, 3:8). God says "the way of man is not in himself: it is not in man that walketh to direct his steps" (see Jer. 10:23). We are depicted as sheep that need a shepherd to guide and lead us throughout our lives. But "all we like sheep have gone astray" (Is. 53:6). We have rejected the restraint of the Shepherd's crook, gone our own way, and are now in deep trouble.

Collective man as well as individual man is in need of God's directions. Cities or nations that set up legislative bodies to devise laws independent of God's law, as history has demonstrated over and over again, are also unable to direct their steps. The hundreds of democracies of ancient Greece were short-lived, averaging about 50 years with the longest lasting a little over 200 years; but they eventually collapsed. Rome had a republic based on allegiance to the city. It lasted longer. Eventually it was supplanted by an impartial form of government which degenerated into a Caesar-centered monarchy, becoming so corrupt that it collapsed when invaded by relatively small barbarian forces. Even Christian Europe fared little better in this respect. Wars and political intrigues litter its history, each petty prince attempting to take control of land and cities held by another. The longest lasting regime was the Byzantine Empire, which held out against the forces of the East for a thousand years. But the best of all of these fell far short of God's standard for what would constitute good government. Freedom and prosperity were very limited conditions afforded only to a relatively small segment of the population. Even America, the great experiment in Christian civil government, is now showing widespread decline. Its founders were greatly influenced by God's law, but despite their pursuing Biblical principles of liberty extensively, later the people as stewards were not able to protect and expand a permanent full sense of it.

History has indeed confirmed man's inability to govern himself. Because of man's innate inability (that is compounded by his sin nature), his attempts to govern himself without regard to God's directions have always led to failure of one sort or another. But God's word has given us sufficient information about how we are to live in this world, including how to structure civil government.

It is specifically the rejection of God's civil laws that has kept the world in the sorry state we saw throughout history and still see today. The absence of these restraints has permitted evil men to rise to positions of power where they have been able to exert influence far greater than their numbers would justify. God's civil laws punished evil men with vigor; His laws did not permit them to live and continue to undermine society. This said, it should be recognized that God's law affords man a great deal of freedom. Of the few hundred laws given by God in the Bible, many do not carry any civil penalties at all, but while instructing men, sentence for infraction is reserved to God Himself either in this life or at the final judgment.

LOVE YOUR NEIGHBOR

The Ten Commandments (see Exod. 20:1–17) are a basic statement of God's law that deals with what is required of everyone. It is composed of two sections: the first four teach us what it means to love God; the last six delineate the meaning of "love your neighbor as yourself." Christ told us that these are the two great commandments on which all the law and the prophets depend (see Matt. 22:35–40). This expression, "the law and the prophets," sends us back to the Old Testament, to the Ten Commandments and their exposition by the prophets God sent to correct the errors of later generations in Israel.

Before we go too much further with this, we need to understand that the Biblical concept of love is very different from the modern usage of the word. It is not a feeling in one's heart so much as the actions that one takes to enhance the well-being of the object of love. To love your neighbor as yourself in the modern sense of a feeling in the heart is beyond human ability. But to do so in the Biblical sense of how he is to be treated is something anyone can do. Likewise, love for God is expressed through obedience to Him, through action rather than only feelings. "Love" in the Bible is an action word.

These two principles—love for God and love for neighbor—constitute the bedrock of civilized society. When each man loves his neighbor, trust increases, the degree to which the force of law is required to maintain contractual obligations is minimized, and free cooperation is enhanced. America's prosperity today stems from the highly developed division of labor, where people cooperate with each other in order to be able to specialize and then share the resultant wealth, which is found in its free-enterprise economy. This in turn is a consequence of the centuries of Christian obedience to God's commandments that preceded it.

Freedom of action, freedom from government coercion, and prosperity all derive from love for neighbor and the self-government it produces in daily life. Without love for neighbor, society disintegrates, laws are multiplied to keep order, and freedom is, of necessity, greatly restricted. As the faith declines, trust is lost, the division of labor cannot be maintained, and both freedom and prosperity diminish accordingly.

Men can only be free and will only truly prosper when they obey this law of love. But without the love of God and a faith that results in obedience to Him, love for neighbor is virtually impossible. Hence, the foundation of both freedom and prosperity is, first of all, love for God. To expect fallen man to love others as he loves himself is akin to belief in the tooth fairy. It is only the love of God, a love that results in obedience, that constrains a man so as to keep him from taking opportunity to enrich himself at his neighbor's expense. As Robert Winthrop said so well: "Men, in a word, must necessarily be controlled either by a power within them or by a power without them; either by the Word of God or by the strong arm of man; either by the Bible or by the bayonet." [21] It is only when men are born of the Spirit, embrace Christ as their Savior and Lord, and love and obey God that the bayonet can be dispensed with.

To love your neighbor as yourself goes far beyond "live and let live." It requires an attitude, a desire to help others in any way you can. The parable of the Good Samaritan illustrates this (see Luke 10:25–37). A lawyer, an expert in God's law, wanted to put boundaries on the law by restricting the range of people that would fall into the class of "neighbor." Christ disappointed him by showing that even a total stranger is a neighbor he should love as he loves himself. In other words, everyone in the world is your neighbor, even people you don't know or may dislike. This principle—and this parable especially—formed the foundation of Christian charity, which was a major factor in the growth and development of Christianity.

We see in these two simple instructions, love for neighbor and love for God, an example of the wisdom and elegant sufficiency of God's law. There are no mountains of civil and criminal statutes such as we have today, statutes that attempt to cover any sort of crime or misdemeanor that anyone could conceive of in any imaginable circumstance. Today's law books are so voluminous and so cryptically worded that few are able to even begin to understand them in any sort of comprehensive sense. God's laws are so few and so easily understood that any literate person can master them with moderate effort. These characteristics of simplicity and conciseness make possible a wide dissemination of legal understanding. This would keep to a minimum the excesses lawyers and politicians are prone to introduce.

When a people have the Holy Spirit sealed in their hearts and are

---

21 Robert Charles Winthrop (1809–1894), American legislator, author, orator, and descendant of Governor John Winthrop, speaking May 28, 1849 at the Annual Meeting of the Massachusetts Bible Society in Boston. *America's God and Country Encyclopedia of Quotations*, William J. Federer, FAME Publishing, 1994, 702.

armed with a thorough knowledge of the Bible and God's law, they become both self-governed and better able to resist the passage of civil laws that contradict God's law. This would ultimately lead to the establishment of communities or a nation of people that govern themselves wherein oppression ceases and freedom permeates the very air they breathe.

CONSEQUENCES

Early on in the history of Israel when God gave His law to that nation through His servant Moses, He clarified what would flow from obedience or disobedience to the laws He gave them: from obedience, blessings flow; from disobedience, curses. Just as Adam and Eve were required to obey God, so were those Israelites, and so are we today. It was and still is: obey and be blessed, or disobey and suffer God's verdict that follows. Freedom of action, free agency was and remains man's prerogative. We are not machines; we are free to choose and are responsible for the consequences that result from our choices.

Blessings

God told ancient Israel and tells us in Deuteronomy 28 that He will bless His people with all sorts of temporal blessings when they obey His commandments. The blessings that flow from obedience (see Deut. 28:1–14) are, in summary:

1. Our fertility and population will increase.
2. The ground will yield good crops.
3. Livestock will be healthy and multiply.
4. Stored goods will not spoil.
5. We will be safe in our homes and fields.
6. We shall defeat our enemies in war.
7. We will remain obedient to God.
8. Other nations shall fear us.
9. We shall prosper in number and in wealth.
10. The work of our hands will be successful and not wasted.
11. We will be lenders to other nations and not borrowers.
12. Our nation will be foremost among nations.

This is a specific list of blessings that pertain to the particular agrarian society that existed in Israel at that time. Today's list might be worded differently but the principle would be the same; every area of life would be blessed. The qualification given in verse one is significant: "if thou shalt hearken diligently unto the voice of the LORD thy God, to observe and to *do all his commandments* which I command thee this day..." [*emphasis added*]. For blessings to be bestowed, *all* God's commandments must be obeyed. Blessings will be withheld or curtailed when a people ignore even one commandment (Jas. 2:10).

Notice that these are primarily national blessings. They apply to individuals also, but it is the nation as a whole that defeats its enemies, that has peace in the land, and enjoys fruitful harvests. It is national obedience that is rewarded. Some number of individuals or families may not be faithful, but if the nation in its laws (and the prosecution thereof), as well as the demeanor of the general population, reflect obedience to God's commandments, all will be blessed.

Much of Scripture has this sort of national or cultural application (Psalm 33:12; Deut. 28). We misread Scripture when we reduce God's workings to the level of the individual only and fail to see the familial, national, and cultural aspects thereof. Today's atomistic overemphasis on the individual's personal faith and personal relationship with God to the neglect of God's dealings with families and larger associations is inconsistent with Scripture. This is not to demean personal salvation or individuality. Scripture recognizes the significance of both the individual and the associations in which he participates.

These words of promised blessing were given through Moses to the people of Israel. Many say that that law and these promises don't apply to us today. But is that so? Does God no longer bless nations that obey Him? Scripture says, "Blessed is the nation whose God is the LORD" (see Ps. 33:12). This is not just Israel but any nation that obeys. In Israel's preparation to enter the promised land, Moses informed Israel that her law would be a model for the nations to emulate (Deut. 4:6). Has God not blessed the Christian nations, especially those that followed the Reformation, far in excess of all other nations in the world? If America reverses its current course and returns to obedience, God's blessing will be restored.

Curses

The flip side, of course, is the curses that are invoked for disobedience (Deut. 28:15–68):

1. The blessings of obedience listed above will be reversed.
2. Plagues and pestilence will come upon us.
3. Our population will diminish until we are all gone.
4. Enemies will be victorious over us.
5. God will no longer hear our prayers.
6. God will send droughts and the land will be destroyed.
7. Our enemies will be strengthened and will defeat us.
8. Our dead bodies will be consumed by birds and beasts.
9. We will become infected with communicable diseases.
10. We will be smitten with insanity, blindness, and heart failure.
11. We will lose all sense of direction and our prosperity will become oppression.
12. Our wives/families, homes, and produce will be taken away from us.
13. Our livestock and work animals shall be taken by our enemies.
14. Our children shall be taken by our enemies, and we shall not be able to get them back.
15. The produce of our fields will be taken by a nation we don't know.
16. We will be driven to madness by what we will see.
17. Our limbs and bodies will become infected with disease.
18. We will be taken into captivity by strange nations and will worship their gods.
19. All other nations shall speak of our downfall.
20. Locusts will consume our crops.
21. Worms shall eat the grapes of our vineyards.
22. Our olive trees shall not produce edible fruit.
23. Locusts shall consume all our trees and fruit.
24. Strangers within the land shall rule over us.
25. They shall lend to us and become heads over us.
26. All these curses shall come because we did not obey God and keep his commandments and laws.
27. Because we did not serve God, we shall become slaves to our enemies until they destroy us.

28. We will be driven to cannibalism when besieged by our enemies and will contend with each other for the flesh of our offspring.

29. The Lord will rejoice to destroy us and reduce us and cause us to be taken off the land he gave us.

30. He will scatter us throughout the nations of the earth where we will serve other gods and find no rest.

31. We will fear for our lives night and day.

32. In the morning we will wish for evening and in the evening we will wish for morning.

33. We shall be sold as slaves by our enemies.

These lists of blessings and curses are often taken with a grain of salt, even by Christians. They sound like the kinds of warnings or threats parents might devise to control their children and so are not taken seriously. But we should remember that they are God's words of warning to His people, and God does not speak frivolously, nor does He employ hyperbole to impress His hearers. If we want to learn from what God tells us, we must take His words seriously and respectfully.

Many more curses are listed than blessings. I suppose that is a reflection of God's wisdom and understanding of the fallen nature of the people He is dealing with. The curses though are not just punishments but are meant as chastisements, intended to provoke repentance on the part of a rebellious people. God worked patiently with that stiff-necked people until they crucified the Son (Matt. 21:33–45). Likewise He has had patience with America but is judging us even now for the many ways we have provoked Him through our continued disobedience. God's word is very clear: obey and be blessed, disobey and suffer the consequences.

God's judgment for disobedience may be delayed for an extended period of time. The blessings God has poured out on America for the obedience rendered by its citizens during the eighteenth and nineteenth centuries are still present in the twenty-first century. God's blessings come at different levels, such as religious, moral, and financial. Each underpins the next and are gained and lost in sequence. America lost most of its religious strength in the nineteenth century, its moral standards in the twentieth, and is now losing its once great wealth and prosperity. This lengthy time frame reflects the fact that God's judgment is not turned on or off in a day or solely at a point in time when He decides enough is enough. He generally operates within the law structure He established and allows it to produce the results He ordains. This applies to God's spiritual, moral, and economic, as well as physical, laws.

Because God controls all things, the consequences are actually God's chastisement for disobedience, but they can also be seen as the logical outcome of failing to obey God's commandments. A nation that disobeys God becomes corrupt and is thereby weakened both economically and militarily. It becomes poor and is easily conquered and oppressed by its enemies. Likewise, the reverse is true of a faithful and obedient nation. All this can be viewed as due directly to its failure to obey God's moral and economic laws rather than as a specific act of God in judgment. Regardless of how one chooses to look at it, though, the outcome of disobedience is loss of freedom, loss of wealth, and a general degradation of life in the disobedient nation.

This characteristic of God's laws containing within themselves the blessings for obedience and curses for disobedience shows us how attuned God's laws are to man's nature and his environment. Because this loving God created man, obedience always increases man's well-being while disobedience diminishes it. This is true for individuals, families, or nations. God's laws are laws that spring from His love for His creatures. In all His laws, God's sovereign will is aligned with man's nature and directed to man's benefit. His curses for disobedience that can lead to repentance and restoration are no less acts of love than are His blessings.

OBEDIENCE

We see that obeying God is all-important; but what constitutes obedience and how do we measure it? Where do we draw the line that defines disobedience?

In the first place, obedience to God requires an accurate understanding of God's commandments and how they apply to us today. Scripture is very clear on both these points, and the average Christian can with some effort answer them for himself. To obey what one believes to be God's commandment but, in fact, is not, is still disobedience. That would not be the disobedience of rebellion against God's law, but the blessings listed above are nevertheless withheld. Whether it is an individual or a nation that is led astray by false teachers, curses rather than blessings are invoked by that disobedience. We see in this how important it is for each believer to guard against any theology that trivializes or negates any of God's commandments. A nation of Biblically astute Christians that work together to protect against the incursions of such false teachings is truly blessed by God.

Secondly, obedience must be total. James tells us that if we disobey any commandment we have disobeyed all: "For whosoever shall keep the whole law, and yet offend in one point, he is guilty of all" (see James 2:10).

That may seem strange on the surface. But when we consider the process that lets us conclude which commandments we think we can safely disobey, we see that we are setting ourselves up as judges of the law. The implication is that the denial of even one commandment displays that the person so doing has placed himself as a judge above the law. He decides, based on whatever standards he wishes to apply, whether this or that commandment is or is not in agreement with his idea of justice. He obeys certain laws because he agrees with them and rejects the rest. So it is not God's law at all that he obeys but his own, self-determined law.

When this is done, the whole of God's law is set aside and our own law substituted in its place. There is only *seeming* or *self-perceived* but no *actual* obedience to any of God's commandments. Any seeming obedience is incidental; we have, as the serpent said to Eve, made ourselves gods, determining for ourselves what is good and what is evil.

We find numerous commandments in Scripture and the question is often asked: Which of these must one obey *today*? Can they be categorized so that we can understand how to obey? To place God's laws into categories not clearly defined in Scripture is to add our own false ideas to them. We must not judge God's laws but rather simply obey them all.

What are the penalties associated with disobeying *some* of them? Scripture teaches us in Matthew 22 that the Pharisees, wanting to know which they had to obey and where they could cut corners, asked this question:

> 36 Master, which is the great commandment in the law?
>
> 37 Jesus said unto him, Thou shalt love the Lord thy God with all thy heart, and with all thy soul, and with all thy mind.
>
> 38 This is the first and great commandment.
>
> 39 And the second is like unto it, Thou shalt love thy neighbour as thyself.

40 On these two commandments hang all the law and the prophets.

The answer addressed their unstated objective, which was to divide the law into mandatory and optional categories. By associating *all* the law and the prophets with these two "greatest" commandments, Christ closed the door to any such notion. His answer was that all of God's laws, both explicit and implicit, are to be obeyed to their fullest extent. He did not permit them (or us) to establish categories that might serve to govern the degree of obedience necessary to each. These two commandments are often held to be a summary of the Ten Commandments but they are both found elsewhere in the Old Testament (see Deut. 6:5 and Lev. 19:18). What Christ says here shows us that not just the Ten Commandments but *all* the Law-Word given by God to Israel is to be obeyed as well.

Another division that can be employed to compromise God's law is between the physical and the spiritual, saying some commandments are merely for our physical, while others are for our spiritual well-being. The latter are taken to be much more important because they are of eternal significance while the former are merely temporal and can be taken lightly. While it is true that the consequences of disobedience vary over a wide range, all commandments and the "general equity" principles underlying case law are still God's Law-Word and still apply, and none can be set aside with impunity. As Christians who subscribe to salvation by grace alone and not works (or a mixture of grace and works as these Pharisees in Matthew 22 did), we obey God because He is God and out of gratitude for His mercy. We do not attempt to seek ways to shortcut God's laws while hoping we're not offending Him too greatly.

This separation of God's laws into physical and spiritual (with its implications of optional and mandatory) carries with it an element of pharisaism. It also displays a tendency toward the Manichaean idea that radically separates body and spirit.[22] God treats us as the whole beings we are and issues commandments that cover all aspects of our body and spirit being. He knows much better than we do what is important for us,

---

22 *Manichaean,* from the doctrine of Manes (216?–276?), a Persian; a mixture of Zorastrian dualism and Christian soteriology—with the soul from Light, seeking to escape from Darkness, the body—and with release through false messiah and renunciation of everything material; was suppressed locally but spread and survived for centuries.

and we need to obey God's commandments simply because they are His commandments without regard to whether they are physical or spiritual. We must remember that we are mere creatures and cannot comprehend the full intent or significance of God's laws.

From Christ's answer to the Pharisees we can see that no one actually obeys any of the commandments in any way even approaching full compliance. In fact, as some have put it, "we all disobey every one of the Ten Commandments every day."[23] This may be an exaggeration, but we must realize that none of us are perfect; we all have a long way to go in the process of sanctification and should strive to be obedient to God in every way.

We read in Proverbs 3:

> 5 Trust in the LORD with all thine heart; and lean not unto thine own understanding.
>
> 6 In all thy ways acknowledge him, and he shall direct thy paths.
>
> 7 Be not wise in thine own eyes: fear the LORD, and depart from evil.
>
> 8 It shall be health to thy navel, and marrow to thy bones.

Because God has given us perception, intelligence, and understanding, we tend to think we can handle whatever comes along. We make decisions and take action very often without a thought of God and God's word, and this is often quite reasonable. The danger, though, is the tendency to think that our understanding is good enough, that we can manage and get by even when our understanding differs from God's. We go astray when we fail to acknowledge Him in *all* our ways. We prosper when we lean *not* on our own understanding and instead trust the Lord with all our hearts.

So, if we are to be governed by God's word as we find it in Scripture, we must obey *all* of God's Law-Word. Whether we, using our own logic, agree with them or not, they are still His laws and binding upon us. The Law-Word of God is His full counsel. It is a *command*-word and not just an optional set of directions we can with impunity choose to follow or disregard as we please. Yes, we can foolishly choose to ignore His word

---

23 Before you jump to the conclusion that this is an excessive exaggeration, see the Westminster Larger Catechism answers to questions 99–149.

but only to our eventual sorrow and chagrin. It is one thing to fail to obey due to weakness, ignorance, or inadvertence, but quite another matter to refuse to obey. Indeed, to reject any of God's laws is to deny the faith.

God's truth, though, is not fallen man's favorite reading. Many objections have been raised against the idea of total obedience, particularly with respect to the Old Testament civil code.

OBJECTIONS

The Sacrificial System

One area of contention is the Old Testament sacrificial system, which the New Testament clearly says was meant only to point to Christ. This tells us that obedience to these commands today consists, not in animal sacrifice, but in recognizing Christ as our sacrifice such as we demonstrate in the practice of Holy Communion. The sacrificial law is not so much done away with as it is fulfilled in Christ. But we now understand its true meaning: that Christ is the final sacrifice or, as John the Baptist said, "the lamb of God" (see John 1:29, 36). The book of Hebrews gives us explicit information regarding this.

Hebrews 9:

> 11 But Christ being come an high priest of good things to come, by a greater and more perfect tabernacle, not made with hands, that is to say, not of this building;
>
> 12 Neither by the blood of goats and calves, but by his own blood he entered in once into the holy place, having obtained eternal redemption for us.
>
> 13 For if the blood of bulls and of goats, and the ashes of an heifer sprinkling the unclean, sanctifieth to the purifying of the flesh:
>
> 14 How much more shall the blood of Christ, who through the eternal Spirit offered himself without spot to God, purge your conscience from dead works to serve the living God?

Hebrews 10:

> 1 For the law having a shadow of good things to come, and not the very image of the things, can never with those sacrifices which they offered year by year continually make the comers thereunto perfect.

2 For then would they not have ceased to be offered? because that the worshippers once purged should have had no more conscience of sins.

3 But in those sacrifices there is a remembrance again made of sins every year.

4 For it is not possible that the blood of bulls and of goats should take away sins.

5 Wherefore when he cometh into the world, he saith, Sacrifice and offering thou wouldest not, but a body hast thou prepared me:

6 In burnt offerings and sacrifices for sin thou hast had no pleasure.

7 Then said I, Lo, I come (in the volume of the book it is written of me,) to do thy will, O God.

8 Above when he said, Sacrifice and offering and burnt offerings and offering for sin thou wouldest not, neither hadst pleasure therein; which are offered by the law;

9 Then said he, Lo, I come to do thy will, O God. He taketh away the first, that he may establish the second.

10 By the which will we are sanctified through the offering of the body of Jesus Christ once for all.

These words plainly tell us that the entire sacrificial system was instituted to point to the coming of the Lamb of God whose blood took away the sins of the world. The blood of bulls and goats could not take away sin but they did serve a purpose: They provided a very visible and sensible image of the seriousness of sin and the death penalty it merited. These Israelites were at least as susceptible to falling into sinful ways of life as we are today. The God-mandated regular repetition of animal sacrifice in Old Testament Israel was a constant reminder—that "the wages of sin is death" (Ro. 6:23), and that a Messiah who would bear the penalty of the sins of all the people would be forthcoming. There was a difference in perspective but no essential difference in faith between the Old and New Testaments. The former looked ahead to the coming of Christ; the latter basks in the glory of His having come and looks forward to His return. The same unchanging law of God that governed the one governs the other. The ceremonial and ritual aspects of God's law were not just set aside as an afterthought; they were sets of practices put in place as temporary measures until the true final sacrifice appeared in Christ Jesus, the Lamb of God.

Where the book of Hebrews speaks of a *change* in the law (see Heb. 7:12), it is related to the High Priesthood of Christ, who was not descended from Aaron. This was, for the believing Jews, a point of contention. They had no problem seeing Christ as prophet and king but had a real problem with His being a priest; after all, He wasn't even a Levite! From their point of view, this was a major change in the law, one which they resisted. The primary thrust of the book of Hebrews was to show them that there was no real change in the original intent; the priesthood of Christ was always God's plan and consistent with the law He gave through Moses. Just as sacrifices were no longer appropriate, so also the priesthood of Christ replaced that of Aaron. Christ was identified as the only mediator between God and man, and the Levitical priesthood, having fulfilled its purpose, was now obsolete.

These passages solidly underscore the continuity that exists between ancient Israel and the church, and between the Old and New Testaments.

God's Law Too Harsh

Another aspect of God's law that has been used by its detractors to demean and disparage it is the seeming harshness of some penal portions of the law—e.g., the death penalty for adultery, repeated crimes, proselytizing to false religions, and even for cursing of parents (Lev. 20:9). They are often held up, even by Christians, as despicable examples of brutal, primitive, and long-dead ideas of justice.

But before we react with aversion to these laws, we need to remember that the Triune God, the God who is love personified (see 1 John 4:8, 16), gave these laws to ancient Israel, His chosen people. God knew that even in this select and highly favored nation there would always be those that would rebel against Him and disobey His commandments. It was important to deal severely with this element to keep it from growing and subverting the whole population. God knew that those Israelites, just as we today, were formed in iniquity and conceived in sin (see Psalm 51:5). He knew that without severe penalties for law-breaking, this element would grow bold and lead the people to become more and more corrupt with the passage of time. God's law deals with man as he really is. It does not attempt to hide his sin nature or put on a good face, one that would be more acceptable to the more sensitive among us.

The crime of murder (what we know as first degree) is a serious enough offense to warrant the death penalty. Why is this so? First, because it is too disruptive to society to be tolerated. If murder were permitted to proliferate, the whole structure of society would be affected, there would be an outcry and a popular clamor for safety. Second, a lesser punishment is inadequate to compensate for the loss of life or act as a deterrent. Murder is often a desperate action. It may be a sudden decision or one carefully thought through. In either case, the individual sees no appropriate alternative for solving his problem other than the taking of a life. Only the real threat of the death penalty is sufficient to restrain the individual in such circumstances. This has been demonstrated to be true over and over again in countless case histories. Likewise, the capital crimes listed in Scripture are offenses, 1) that are too disruptive to society to be tolerated, and 2) for which a lesser penalty would not be sufficient.

The only alternative to self-discipline and self-government is external constraint by the force of government backed up by the authority of law enforcement with its threat of jail and/or prison. God's formula leads to a moral, self-disciplined, and free population. The alternative is an immoral, self-seeking people that cannot live in peace without the constant reminder of the heavy hand of government ready to punish the lawbreaker. In addition, government regulations would be expanded to the point that they become an oppressive burden everyone must bear and all become the slaves of the regulators. To quote Robert Winthrop once again: "Men, in a word, must necessarily be controlled either by a power within them or by a power without them; either by the Word of God or by the strong arm of man; either by the Bible or by the bayonet."[24] God's law makes freedom possible; without it, the force of law eventually strips away all liberty. Government cannot be eliminated; it just shifts from an internal (self-controlled) to an external (civil) form.

---

24 Robert Charles Winthrop (see footnote 21 p. 56).

One of the practices much condemned by critics of God's law is that of stoning as a form of execution. It is looked upon as an archaic and brutal practice that has no place in today's civilized world. But God did not establish it for ancient Israel for no reason. While most Christian authorities agree that stoning isn't appropriate today, we should recognize that that method of execution had some positive effects that are lacking in our present forms of execution, such as:

First, it was a public action in which the victims and the entire local community participated. The execution was not only visible to the entire population, but all adults were expected to pick up and throw a stone at the condemned person. This meant that the general public was *involved* in the process. It was not done behind closed doors before a very small group of witnesses, so easy to ignore by most. Everyone was virtually forced to not only witness the death, but to be a contributor to the agony and suffering of the convicted person. An execution was a very serious and a very *personal* matter, one not left to others, to be easily pushed into the background and forgotten as it is today. The fact that children saw a very graphic illustration of the consequences of crime surely discouraged much crime.

Second: Also, the law required that the witnesses who testified against the criminal were to throw the first stones (see Deut. 17:2–7). This, coupled with the law that inflicted upon a perjurer the same punishment that would have been due to the defendant had he been found guilty, would have significantly reduced the incidence of perjury. Witnessing in a court of law was a very serious and personal matter, not something to be taken lightly or with little thought. The consequences of crime were elevated and made very visible, not hidden and remote as it is today.

Modern man is no better than the ancient Israelites, and we are just as much in need of harsh laws to control the tendency to lawlessness that is in all our hearts. This is especially true of unbelievers who were then, and still are, very much under these laws. God's law is not just for believers—*all* are subject to it, and, sooner or later, all persons outside of Christ will come under its condemnation. Our loving God, who knows us far better than we know ourselves, has in His mercy given us laws that are needful for us. Due to today's pitiful lack of Biblical understanding, they may at first seem unduly severe; but we must remember that He is our Father and we are the rebellious children He still loves. His desire is our salvation and the well-being of our society and He knows what kind of medicine to prescribe for it.

Let's not be unruly and disobedient children, and let's not try to be more righteous than the God who is the living definition of righteousness. These seemingly harsh laws are, in actuality, highly benevolent and full of mercy and love, a love we can't even begin to comprehend.

Promoting False Religions

God's law requires the death penalty for anyone proselytizing people into false religions which deny the God of the Bible and His ways (see Deut. 13:6–11). Why? It is because such activity is subversive to the very foundation of government and constitutes treason against society. Without faith in God, the whole system crumbles and falls apart. Most modern nations consider treason against the state a serious enough crime to warrant the death penalty. To speak against God in a society that is utterly dependent on faith in God constitutes sedition against that society. As an act of treason, it also warrants capital punishment.

Please notice though that this law does not authorize forced conversion; there is no civil law against worship of other gods. Anyone in ancient Israel could believe in and worship any god he pleased, provided he did so privately and kept his faith to himself. God reserves judgment of such a person to Himself in His own time. God sees the heart; we do not. We may not judge anyone for what is in his heart. Only by what a person does or says can we judge or condemn him. It is only a person who *takes action* to undermine the faith of the nation that could be tried for treason and become subject to the death penalty.

God knew very well that there would always be potential traitors and therefore placed this harsh but necessary constraint on their ability to propagate their heresies. Christian civil societies that fail to implement this injunction are exposed to subversion and eventual takeover by alien faiths.

Objection to this law is primarily from unbelievers who desire the freedom to practice and propagate their unbelief and antagonism to God, and secondarily from many that see as unfair any attempt to restrict religious practice to a single faith. The latter issue is addressed later under the heading of Pluralism. We need to recognize also that this law cannot be instituted in any society that is not already predominantly Christian in character and is overwhelmingly appreciative and supportive of the need to implement God's law as the law of the land. To attempt to do so by force, as is being tried in Muslim countries today, is futile and doomed to failure. It is also contradictory to the teaching of Scripture itself where we see that acceptance is voluntary. The whole nation of Israel accepted and ratified the law of God as presented to them through Moses (see Exod. 19:3–7).

In ancient Israel, God's chosen people were very much a diverse company. Just as today, there were believers and unbelievers living side by side. God established this law code to insure the perpetuation of the faith. He knew what was in the hearts of His subjects, the in-born tendency to follow Satan's temptation to be as God. He knew that the people would never love their neighbors as themselves unless they also loved God with all their hearts. He also knew that some would rebel openly against Him and that they would draw others away from the faith if they were permitted to do so—hence the seemingly harsh penalties for open disobedience. They were harsh toward offenders but kind toward the people at large; and that served to keep the law of God alive in the land, which is the greatest blessing the nation could ever receive. Without these laws that punished religious dissension with death, the culture would have declined rapidly into a godless society, as indeed, did occur whenever the laws were relaxed.

America is now on a similar trajectory. Society is rapidly moving away from the Christian faith. Had Americans after the founding generation the wisdom and courage to continue to insist on obedience to all of God's laws, had they been more thorough and successful in establishing and maintaining these laws as the basis of their civil laws, this might not be the case today. Humanism would not have been able to undermine and then take control of the culture as it has. Our homes and schools would be teaching God's word to our youth and countless millions of Americans would have been spared wasted lives and the anguish of an eternity in hell.

Indeed, obedience to God's laws results in an overflowing superfluity of blessings. Disobedience is foolishness in the extreme.

Disobedience to Parents

The law-penalty in Deuteronomy 21:18–21 is often cited as a test case in arguments intended to disparage God's law. They picture a child that has perpetrated some minor infraction of the family's rules that is to be stoned for his disobedience. Though this is an extreme example, that is a gross distortion of the facts. This is no small child; it is an incorrigible older person that has no respect for others, even his own parents. The parents take him to the gate and say to the elders of their city, "our son is stubborn and rebellious, he will not obey our voice; he is a glutton, and a drunkard," so then he is judged by the whole community as being beyond redemption. He is well on his way toward a life of crime.

What principles of law should we draw from this particular case? God considers that the offense in this one extreme case warranted the same punishment as murder. On what basis do we reduce the penalty to a slap on the wrist or less? Are we so much better behaved today than the Israelites of old? We can claim, as many do, that ancient Israel no longer exists and its laws expired with it. This is a defective argument. But even if it were true, God did give such a law to that people at that time. Why? We can follow Marcion[25] and say that there are two Gods: the harsh Jehovah of the Old Testament who demanded punishment, and the loving Christ of the New Testament who exhibited mercy and grace. But that is to place Christianity on its head, denying that God is One and that He changes not (see Mal. 3:6; Heb. 13:8). We must inquire as to why God would give such a law to the nation He loved and favored above all nations. Could it be that God considered this law to be a blessing to Israel?

Is extreme disobedience to parents so trivial an offense that it doesn't merit a civil penalty? Actually, it should be considered as a most serious crime, one that represents a major threat to society. An undisciplined population is a breeding ground for lawlessness, crime, and numerous other forms of evil. A child requires more watching than an adult does because his ability for self-governance is not yet fully developed. His total focus is on himself; the well-being of others is often immaterial to him. He has not yet been trained to live in righteousness. An adult who still lacks self-control is a constant danger to everyone around him. He cannot

---

25 *Marcion* of Sinope, an early anti-Judaic Gnostic-Christian bishop, whose followers formed a sect; he was excommunicated by the early church fathers.

be permitted to participate in the kind of free society God's law provides.

We also should appreciate that this law has a very positive effect on the authority and concomitant responsibility given to the family. Education is a family responsibility that begins at a very young age and continues even after the son or daughter is married and becomes a part of a new family. This responsibility is a very heavy one, especially in a society that grants individuals the degree of freedom we see in God's law. In such a society, parental authority is essential.

We read in Proverbs:

> He that spareth his rod hateth his son: but he that loveth him chasteneth him betimes (13:24).

> Foolishness is bound in the heart of a child; but the rod of correction shall drive it far from him (22:15).

Undisciplined, disobedient children grow up to be criminals or, even worse, they poison society with their infectious, self-centered, "what's in it for me" philosophy. We like to think of our children as innocent and basically good, but that is very wrong and very unbiblical. We are all born in sin and need no instruction in it. It is only training in righteousness leading to salvation in Christ that can correct this inborn old nature Adam cursed us with. The "rod of correction" can be thought of as the price of freedom. Without it parental authority is compromised, child training loses effectiveness, and we are left with a godless society, a society of people who lack self-discipline and cannot be permitted the kind of liberty God would have us enjoy.

The necessity for an early education in morals and Godliness requires that this responsibility rests with the family. In fact, civilization as we know it today is still very dependent on strong families, families that inculcate into the youth the precepts and principles of godly living. Ancient Israel was just such a society; civil government was miniscule in size and scope. It was maintained by a tax of a meager one-half shekel per year per adult man. The "church" of that day did not have any delegated power in civil affairs. The family governed everything else.

Consider also if there were any parents driven to the point of taking the extreme action of delivering offspring to civil court, they would necessarily consider themselves abject failures in their training and disciplining of that child. Considering their natural love for their son, it would have been the last resort. They would, without doubt, have given their son many chances to correct his behavior and would have tried every possible solution before taking this final and irrevocable step. It would have been taken only if he actually was utterly incorrigible and beyond redemption.

But many today would be quick to point out that there are parents who really abuse their children. How can such parents be awarded absolute power of life and death over them?

First of all, the parents did not hold that power. This is a civil offense. The parents initiate the action, but there must be other witnesses and it is the elders—the civil court—who must judge and convict the offender. Fathers were not given the right to slay their sons as was the case in ancient Rome. If the elders saw any tendency toward vindictiveness in the parents, they would likely have taken a more lenient action such as placing the offender in the care of another family for a period of time.

Secondly, this law needs to be taken in context with the kind of society God gave the nation of Israel. It is part and parcel with the command to love God and love your neighbor, a concept very far removed from what we see operating today. In a society governed by God's laws, those parents would themselves have been brought up as self-governing, God-honoring, responsible individuals, and the incidence of cases involving this sort of action would have been extremely rare. Actually, there are no cases of such action reported anywhere in Scripture.

Law Written in the Heart

Some assert that these laws are no longer in force today because Christians now have God's law written in their hearts:

> But this shall be the covenant that I will make with the house
> of Israel; After those days, saith the LORD, I will put my law
> in their inward parts, and write it in their hearts; and will be
> their God, and they shall be my people (Jer. 31:33).

But this does not invalidate the law; it is still *God's* law that is written in their hearts. Now what law would Jeremiah have been referring to other than God's Law-Word as found in the Old Testament? We must remember that God does not change, He doesn't give one law at one time and another later on. God through Jeremiah was speaking to the nation of

Israel when He spoke these words. When God said "I will put *my law* in their inward parts," He couldn't have been referring to any law other than the law He had given Israel. Nor could He have been referring to a subset of that law, as many of today's Christian leaders would have us believe. So, does this mean that true Christians today have the entire law of God written in their hearts and have no need to study and learn it? But most Christians are uninformed of even the principles, much less the details, of God's law; so what exactly does this mean?

The difference between God's people today and Israel of old is that the enabling Holy Spirit has been widely distributed and not given only to a limited few. He is present in the hearts of all God's people, everyone who has been born again (Rom. 8:9). They have hearts of flesh and not stone because the Holy Spirit has opened their blind eyes and is showing them what is true and right and real (Rom. 8:4). It is the work of the Holy Spirit in the heart that brings a *desire to obey* God's law.

The presence of the Spirit does not preclude the need to study and learn what God has to teach us from His word. If it did, there would be no need to study Scripture and all Christians would be in total agreement as to what it says and means. What the Spirit does, in fact, is instill in our hearts a desire to study, a desire to learn God's law more perfectly. It is this studious assimilation and practice of God's Law-Word that constitutes growth in Christian maturity.

The Holy Spirit in the heart, the born-again experience, is the essence of the new covenant Jeremiah wrote about, the difference between old Israel and Christians today. God writes His law in our hearts in the sense that it is now our *heartfelt desire* to obey that law. But in any event, God's writing the law on our hearts has not eliminated the need for law. Christians are still plagued by the old nature; their flesh is prone to wandering from God and they need both the understanding and the restraining effect of God's law to keep from sinning. Also, the necessity for God's law among unbelievers is much greater, being in principle the same as for unbelievers in ancient Israel.

Law and Grace

What about the passages that tell us that we are not under law but under grace? Let's look at Romans chapter 6:

14 For sin shall not have dominion over you: for ye are not under the law, but under grace.

15 What then? shall we sin, because we are not under the law, but under grace? God forbid.

16 Know ye not, that to whom ye yield yourselves servants to obey, his servants ye are to whom ye obey; whether of sin unto death, or of obedience unto righteousness?

Doesn't this passage clearly state that the law does not apply to Christians? There are two problems with this conclusion:

First, the unfounded dichotomy proposed is "law versus grace." In what sense are grace and law opposites? To say one is under grace instead of under law, in the sense that the law no longer applies to him, is illogical. It is only because he is under the judgment of the law that a judge can administer grace. Grace is the alternative to judgment and punishment and is only possible in the presence of law. They can only be opposites in the sense that a judge, or anyone having the power to do so, might graciously pardon a convicted criminal and free him from the full judgment and sentence that would be due him otherwise. It is legal judgment versus grace, not law versus grace. Grace does not set the law aside; it extends leniency in special cases. A judge's grace is not the same as God's grace. God transferred our guilt to His Son, something no judge can do. But it is clear that without law, there can be no grace. It is law *and* grace.

Second, in the next verse Paul says that God forbids sin. But sin is the breaking of the law (see 1 John 3:3–6); so to not sin is to keep the law. This may seem to be a contradiction but when we understand "not under the law" to mean not under the condemnation of the law, it all makes sense. When Christ died on the cross, He bore the penalty of the law for all the sins of all believers. They are no longer under the law because the penalty of the law no longer hangs over their heads. They are free to sin or to obey but those who are true believers—those for whom Christ died and who have been born again by the Holy Spirit—in their inner man have a compelling tendency to obey God. They do so out of gratitude and reverence, not fear of judgment. They are able to obey, however imperfectly, because sin no longer has dominion over them as it does over those who are under the law (see verse 14). In Romans 7, Paul explains this strange effect: how this dominion of sin prevents those who are under the law from keeping the law.

This is one of the marvels of God's salvation. He gave His law through Moses to His creatures—a law they needed in order to live (see Lev. 18:5). But they rejected Him, came under the dominion of sin and lost the ability to obey His life-giving law (Rom. 8:8). But, in His love and mercy, He sent His Son to bear the penalty of their sin upon His own shoulders. This freed them from the dominion of sin and enabled them to obey the commandments that were previously beyond their ability to obey. God's ways are truly greater than our ways and far beyond our comprehension. But no matter how hard we try, as many antinomians (those opposed to the Old Testament law for today) do, we cannot make these passages say that Christians are no longer required to obey God's law.

Today, many think of grace and law as alternatives with respect to salvation. But Scripture never speaks of salvation by law. Salvation, both before and after Christ, has always been by faith and not by works of the law. Much of the opposition to law today stems from the erroneous idea that salvation before Christ was by obedience to the law. But that is not possible for, as Paul writes, "all have sinned, and come short of the glory of God" (see Rom. 3:23). In other words, no one has ever obeyed the law so well as to merit salvation through perfect obedience. If salvation before Christ was by law, then no one could have been saved, and this, as we see in the long list of the faithful found in Hebrews 11, was clearly not the case. We are saved by the grace of God because we were first under the judgment of the law and subject to its penalties. If we were not under God's law, then we would have no need for grace or salvation.

Where James writes in chapter 2 of justification by works, the thrust of his words is that works of law provide evidence of true faith. "I will show thee my faith by my works" and "Ye see then how that by works a man is justified, and not by faith only" (see James 2:18, 24). He does not use the word "justified" in the same sense Paul does. It is justification before men (evidential justification), not before God (forensic justification), that is intended: "I will show *thee* my faith."

Parenthetically, this is one more passage that underscores the fact that Christians are required to obey God's law including the Old Testament law, which is the law James would have been referring to in this passage. If faith without works is dead (see chapter 2, especially verses 18, 20, and 26), then "works," in other words *active obedience* to God's Law, is required. The "works" do not save; they are an evidence of true faith. Implicit though in the requirement of works as evidence is the necessity of obedience to God's entire Law-Word—by Christians!

Abuse of the Law

Some will say that such a law would be subject to much abuse. They see witch-hunts initiated to punish the innocent and benefit the few. As attested to by the Spanish Inquisition and other instances of abuse, this is a real problem and a valid objection. It should not be brushed off but requires serious attention.

We also should realize that because man is what he is, all laws are abused to some extent. The rich and powerful have exerted their influence and exploited the poor and weak in every form of government that has ever existed. Among the worst of all forms of abusive governments have been democracies. Rule by the people has no record of longevity beyond a hundred years or so. They have often degenerated into tyrannical despotism with great rapidity. America's founding fathers abhorred the idea of establishing a democracy and established a constitutional republic to prevent that.

The utility, efficacy, and proper execution of God's law are dependent on the faith and diligence of the entire population. It can only be implemented in a God-fearing, God-obeying culture. In such an environment the incidences of abuse would be limited and, as the depth and extent of unbelief was reduced, would decrease further with time. A godly population—one that knows God's laws, is intent on obeying them, and also has the freedom of action it provides—would act to correct and prevent abuse wherever it arose. The kinds of despotism we see in the governments of the world today would never be able to arise, much less prosper.

Ultimately we must say that God is God and He knows far better than we what sort of government we need. He is a loving God and would not lead us astray or hurt us. This merciful God that sent His Son to die in our place has given us these laws to live by. Because we are sinful, abuses will occur; but we cannot do better than to forsake our own understanding and follow God's direction in all things, including law and government.

The Law Is Impractical

When one looks at the history of religion in America, a once strongly Christian nation, it's easy to become discouraged about ever being able to establish civil government according to God's law anywhere. It would seem that with all the diversity of opinion within Christianity it would be ludicrous to expect any agreement at all, much less agreement on God's law. Man is basically sinful and self-oriented and always resists controls of any kind. As we see from Psalm 2, natural man fights against what he sees as the imposition of a law that restricts his freedom to sin. So how can a program that includes as controversial a provision as God's law ever get off the ground, much less endure for any length of time?

The difficulties associated with the implementation of God's law are many and varied. Some of the questions that arise are:

1. What is a false religion?

2. Who decides what constitutes the true faith?

3. How do the many denominations of Christian churches fit into this scheme?

4. How are differences of opinion regarding interpretation to be resolved?

5. How can we provide for change as we learn and develop a better understanding of God's word?

6. How can we avoid the kinds of excesses found in non-Biblical religions such as Islam?

And considering the doubtless many other such difficulties that lie in the path, implementing God's law might appear to be a formidable and seemingly impossible task. We might be led to throw in the towel and give up trying, but that would be the worst possible choice. It would require that we deliberately close our eyes to God's word in this particular area or forsake the Christian faith altogether. Indeed, the latter is what is happening by degrees all across the world today. But to ignore the plain teaching of God's word at any point is just as bad. As James tells us (2:10), to disobey at one point is to disobey all. So this also would lead to the eventual abandonment of the Christian faith on earth.

But if we want to remain Christians and obey God in the faithful and complete sense that He commands, these questions and many others will need to be dealt with. This is clearly a very large task that will occupy many minds for a significant length of time. All that we can say at this point is that the guiding principle should be that God's word always governs. The principles found in God's word must govern the establishment process as well as provide the laws themselves. We need to recognize that we are creatures and not gods and cannot outdo God. Any attempt to do so always leads to error and failure.

In addition, we must be extremely careful to avoid falling into the trap of thinking we can improve on God's laws. We may very logically and very sincerely believe that a tweak here or there would enhance what God has given us. These kinds of suggestions should be taken as warning flags alerting us to the dangers that lie ahead.

The only safeguard against any of these pitfalls is a Biblically astute population, one that will correct deviations from the plain meaning of Scripture. Sadly, at this writing, we are a great distance away from this happy circumstance, so full implementation of God's word can only be a goal for the future. Much preparatory work needs to be done. The primary prerequisite is a God-fearing, God-honoring, and God-obeying society, one that truly places God's word first. We do not have this today, but we will someday and it must begin somewhere. Why not let it begin here and now, and with you?

We need to keep in mind what all of Scripture demonstrates and the prophet told us: "The way of man is not in himself: it is not in man that walketh to direct his steps" (see Jer. 10:23). Implementation may be a difficult challenge, but we need to understand that there is no viable alternative to God's law. Without it, we are condemned to one experimental failure after another.

8

THEOLOGICAL DRIFT

THEOLOGY, Biblical and Christian Theology in particular, is the systematic study from the Bible of the existence, character, and attributes of God, the doctrines we are to believe and duties we are to practice. Bible reading and study are essential to the maintenance of a Christian culture. Of all the possible causes of the decline in Christian influence, the lack of a good understanding of God's word is foremost. Too many Christians today reject doctrine as too dry and too dismal a subject. "Give me Christ" they say and "keep your doctrine." But without God's word, there is no Christianity. Without the Bible, each individual invents a Christ of his own making and becomes an idolater. We see an example of this in the WWJD (What Would Jesus Do?) fad that was popular among Christian youth. They wore bracelets bearing WWJD and attempted to do what they believed Jesus would do in situations that arose. But typically their actions were what they personally believed Jesus would do. In violation of the second commandment, they set up as an idol their own particular idea of Jesus based on their feelings and notions. But Jesus said He does only the Father's will; in other words, He obeys God's law. Instead of WWJD, it should be DWJD—Do What Jesus Did (and said)—simply obey God's law.

It is unpleasant and can be very difficult to have to go back and question ideas we have held to be true for a long time. But the current world situation tells us that something has gone very wrong, and—if we are to be faithful servants of Christ—we should be willing to re-examine ourselves and what we have believed to see if some of the problem, perhaps, indeed lies with us. We must do this in the light of God's word itself, not just what we have always assumed it to mean in the past. We cannot leave any stone unturned in the quest for truth. Christianity is in trouble and if we want to find out why, we must be ready to question and examine our assumptions regardless of how long we've held them and how many others may agree with us.

This is not to say we should compromise any of the essentials of the Christian faith. The omnipotent, omniscient, omnipresent Triune God created heaven and earth and all things in it. The Bible is His word and is inspired truth from cover to cover. Christ died on a real cross and only His blood atones for sin. One is saved by faith alone and not by works of righteousness. Without compromising any of these fundamental truths, let's go to the Scriptures and see if we can discover where we may have lost our way.

The intent here is not to critique the diverse and devious paths taken by liberal and fringe-element theology; it is rather to consider a few of the critical areas where almost all, even some of the most-conservative schools of thought, have gone astray.

SOVEREIGNTY

Sovereignty is defined as dominion, rule, power, or authority. The sovereign of any society is the ultimate lawgiver of that society. Today, sovereignty is claimed only by the state. We speak of sovereign states or sovereign nations that claim this authority. In earlier times, the clan leader or tribal chief was the sovereign lawgiver in his society. For example, Louis XIV of France said *"l'etat, c'est moi"* (the state, it's me). He saw himself as Sovereign; law sprang from his mind and his lips.

In the Christian West, sovereignty was generally understood to belong to God alone. The authority of kings was considered to be derivative from God and subordinate to God. This was affirmed by the Council of Chalcedon (A.D. 451) when it declared of Christ, the God-man, that His human nature was distinct and separate from His divinity. In other words, they underscored the premise that men could not become gods or participate to any degree in the divine nature. Sovereignty was expelled from earth and restricted to heaven.

This was an important milestone in Christian history. It provided the theological foundation for Christian liberty and led to a degree of freedom for the common man never before seen in history. How so? Rulers could no longer, as many of the ancient emperors did, claim divinity—and the sovereignty concomitant with it. They could not say, "My word is law because I am a god," rather, they had to resort to claiming to be God's representative and merely the administrator of His law. Now, to be an administrator is a far cry from being a sovereign ruler. An administrator is required to justify his decisions and actions from his sovereign's words or instructions. If adhered to, this greatly curtails his ability to rule in an unjust manner and extends liberty to the citizenry.

In the Christian world, the decisions and laws set by kings could be and often were challenged by church officials based on Scripture. The Pope had much influence and real power in that he could order an interdict and shut down all church services in a nation. Pope Innocent III did this in 1207 when King John of England refused to accept Stephen Langton, the man the Pope had selected, to be Archbishop of Canterbury. The effect was dramatic; all churches were closed and no baptisms, weddings, or funerals were held for more than a year. The outcry was so great that even this stubborn King eventually had to give ground, and, in 1215, submitted and signed the Magna Charta, an agreement to surrender the kingdom of England to "God and the Saints Peter and Paul." Because the common people understood that sovereignty belonged to God only, the power of kings was limited and at least a measure of freedom was preserved.

A serious impairment to this principle of sovereignty came from within the church itself in the form of doctrinal heresy. It originated with Pelagius, a fifth-century figure who denied the doctrine of original sin. Pelagius claimed that man is basically good and morally unaffected by the Fall. This teaching was fought by Augustine and rejected by the church. But not long after, the church adopted a variant of the original teaching called semi-pelagianism where salvation became the cooperative effort of God and man. This toehold on man's sovereignty was retained until the Reformation. The Reformers rejected it; but, soon after, Jacob Arminius resurrected a similar heresy. In a desperate effort to retain some degree of sovereignty for man, he taught that salvation was by faith in Christ but that it was man who decided whether or not to accept it.

The Arminian doctrine was rejected in 1618 at the Synod of Dordt (also Dort or Dordrecht) but it has revived since and is now a prevalent teaching in many evangelical churches. It effectively places God at man's mercy. He is pictured seated in heaven, having sent His Son to die for sinful man, wringing His hands and hoping His beloved creatures will accept His salvation. God makes salvation available but it is man who decides to accept the offer or not. In this scenario, the final determiner of who is saved and who is lost is sovereign man.

Sadly, the concept that God is the only sovereign has been all but lost. Today, virtually everyone, even Christians, have accepted the premise that nations are sovereign and can formulate their own laws independent of God. This has led to a great expansion of rules and regulations and much loss of individual freedom throughout the world. The removal of this obstacle to sovereignty cleared the way for the rich and powerful to take control of governments, converting republics and democracies into their personal, self-serving oligarchies. As a consequence, freedom—around the world and especially in America—is now evaporating at an accelerating rate.

The concept of God as the only sovereign power, the only final source of law, must be restored before we can make any real progress toward establishing a Christian culture and regaining the liberty we once enjoyed.

God's Law

At each step in the historic progression from Adam to Noah, to Abraham, to Christ, believers were given increasingly more knowledge since each had the experience of previous failures and better tools and understanding with which to work. God gave them the opportunity to build on what they had before, but, unfortunately, that is not what has been done recently. God gave His law in the Old Testament, but too many Christians today, instead of building on it, have abandoned God's law. Instead of upholding that law as Christ did, they choose to believe that the law God gave in the Old Testament has been abrogated and passed away with the nation. But this assertion has no basis since both Christ and the Apostle Paul emphatically reaffirmed the God's entire Law-Word (see Matthew 5:17–19; Romans 1:32; 3:19, 31; 7:7, 12, 16, 22, 25). These contemporary Christians refer to ancient Israel as a theocracy, which means "rule by God." By implication, they mean that, for some strange reason, rule by God is not applicable to Christians today. But if God does not rule us, we must be ruled by men unconstrained by God, which is far worse. Rule by men apart from God is a disaster. It is only because some portions of God's law have been present in man's laws that total disaster has been averted.

This setting aside of God's law has many disturbing implications. In today's churches, there are many who believe in God but reject His law. Their theologians and pastors have told them that God's law is obsolete and doesn't apply to us today and they act accordingly. Without an unshakable standard of right versus wrong, they begin to slip into wrong thinking, bad habits, and sinful behavior patterns. They see their children drifting away from the faith but don't understand why. They fail to discern the connection between the waywardness of their children and their own disobedience.

But today's youth, being less encumbered by tradition, see the inconsistencies in their parent's faith and reject it altogether. Perhaps without full comprehension, they sense that a god without a law is really no god at all. Instead of giving them direction, meaning, and purpose for their lives, such a god leaves his followers to figure life out for themselves. Over time and across generations, a lawless god is seen to be useless and fades into oblivion. This fading-out of God's relevance has been going on in Christianity for more than a century.

Another implication is that, as a result of the loss of God's law, Christians do not have a law system they can offer to the world. All that is left are platitudes such as "traditional values," "family values," and such. One seldom hears "thus saith the Lord" except in a church sermon, and that rarely. Christians offer resistance to change, but few today ever consider the possibility of bringing forth the positive assertion that God's law ought to be the foundation of civil law. They may attempt to offer a subset of God's word as a guiding principle, but when they themselves declare portions of His word irrelevant and inapplicable today, they are limited to offering it piecemeal or as merely good advice. Advice can be taken or rejected at will, so it loses authority and becomes ineffective.

A few decades ago, common citizens often voiced the idea that there was a "higher law," one that stood above the Constitution or any law devised by man. Today this is unheard of; why? The excuse offered is that the Old Testament law has been abrogated by Christ and that Christians in this age go to Christ and the New Testament for guidance. But the New Testament does not provide a specific law code and Christ always sent us back to Old Testament law for clarification and direction. Consider His words from the Sermon on the Mount:

We read in Matthew 5:

> 17 Think not that I am come to destroy the law, or the prophets: I am not come to destroy, but to fulfill.
>
> 18 For verily I say unto you, Till heaven and earth pass, one jot or one tittle shall in no wise pass from the law, till all be fulfilled.
>
> 19 Whosoever therefore shall break one of these least commandments, and shall teach men so, he shall be called the least in the kingdom of heaven: but whosoever shall do and teach them, the same shall be called great in the kingdom of heaven.

The law that Jesus refers to here was the only law recognized as belonging to Israel at that time. The expression *law and Prophets* refers to the entire Old Testament, the Scripture of that day. Some say that the word *fulfill* here means that, since Christ fulfilled the law for us, we no longer need to obey it. But that is truly grasping at straws. To fulfill is to obey in every respect, which is exactly what He and only He—the one and only sinless person who ever lived—did. Christ also said that this law in all its detail, jots and tittles included, would not pass away until the end of the world. To whom could He have been speaking when He said that whoever breaks the least of these commandments would be least in the kingdom of heaven and those that obey will be greatest in the kingdom of heaven? Who are or will be the residents of the kingdom of heaven other than true believers? How can this mean anything other than that Christians are to obey all of these laws—not just the Ten Commandments but God's entire Law-Word—today.

We read in Isaiah 42:

> 1 Behold my servant, whom I uphold; mine elect, in whom my soul delighteth; I have put my spirit upon him: he shall bring forth judgment to the Gentiles.

2 He shall not cry, nor lift up, nor cause his voice to be heard in the street.

3 A bruised reed shall he not break, and the smoking flax shall he not quench: he shall bring forth judgment unto truth.

4 He shall not fail nor be discouraged, till he have set judgment in the earth: and the isles shall wait for his law.

This passage speaks of Christ and the coming universal acceptance of His law, which will judge and govern the Gentiles. We see that "the isles," i.e., the entire world, will "wait for His law." It is not just sweetness and light but a *law* that He will bring, one the world is waiting for. As we saw in the Matthew passage above, this is the same unchanging law that God gave through the Old Testament.

Let's look at another passage that illustrates the same principle. John tells us that the definition of sin is "the transgression of the law" (see 1 John 3:4). Here again we must ask, what law is the apostle referring to? John had no law and could have been speaking of no law other than the law as given by God. Now, if sin is defined as a transgression of the law, and Christians are not to sin, then Christians must obey God's law as it stood in James's day. The logic is irrefutable: Except for the ceremonial laws, which expired with the coming of Christ as the final sacrifice, the Old Testament law is still in force today.

The Puritan and Presbyterian founders of this country, following the Reformers, understood the great need for the nation's laws to be based on God's word. This is in keeping with the Reformation concept of the three uses of the law: 1) To restrict the ungodly so that we might live peaceable lives, 2) to show what sin is and to lead one to Christ, and 3) to be the rule of life for the godly. The intent here is not to give countenance to a man-centered pseudo-theocracy such as is found in Islam's Sharia law. In a Biblical, God-centered law system, each man has a copy of the law in his hand and the power of the governing agency is necessarily limited thereby. Man is made free because Christ is the only king and He is in heaven, not on earth. There is no power on earth that can alter or override His word. This view of law is reflected in the nation's documents. In fact, the Constitution itself is not so much a book of laws as merely a procedural document defining the structure and limits of the federal government. The law for early Americans was assumed to be the Bible and the courts were expected to apply the principles found in God's word in their decisions. Until late in the nineteenth century, it was common practice for judges to read an applicable portion of Scripture before sentencing convicted persons. Their judgment was not based so much on statutes or precedents as on God's word.[26]

The situation today differs markedly in that the Reformed segment of the church is no longer even a significant minority much less a majority of the population and cannot dictate its wishes to the legislators. But how should we respond to this? Should we redefine our theology to have it conform more comfortably to the prevailing conditions? No, we cannot and must not do any such thing! We must declare the whole truth, even when it is painful and costly to do so. Too much depends upon it to do otherwise. This world is in desperate need of God's law and it is Christians—as salt and light—who have been called to uphold and champion the establishment of that law.

The prevailing view among evangelical ministries is that all that is needed to restore liberty in America is the proclamation of the Gospel. They claim that as more and more people are saved, popular sentiment will swing away from selfish consumption and toward fiscal responsibility; and, in turn, the size and scope of government control over individuals will diminish accordingly and freedom will be restored. This view is deficient in that it ignores God's law. These saved Christians must also turn from their wicked ways and obey God before He will heal their land (see 2 Chron. 7:14). The salvation of *the individual* lies in Christ, who said "ye must be born again." But the salvation of *the nation* lies in the application of God's law to the culture.

THE END TIMES

Is Satan so powerful that we can't overcome him without the physical presence of the Lord on our side? Isn't God above all His creatures, Satan included? Didn't he need to seek permission from God before he could trouble Job? Doesn't God exercise and accomplish all His will in all things? And aren't we told that Christ is now seated at the right hand of God where He will remain until all His enemies are made a footstool for His feet (see

26 R. J. Rushdoony, *Law and Liberty*. Vallecito, CA: Ross House Books, 1984, 2009, 112.

Acts 2:35; Heb. 1:13; 10:12–13)? These enemies of Christ are not just spiritual beings, i.e., Satan and his demonic, fallen angels; His enemies include every person who denies Christ in this world. Surely the subjugation of Christ's enemies must include those on earth as well as elsewhere. And, if the subjugation is to be accomplished while Christ sits at God's right hand, doesn't that imply it will be completed before His bodily return, and not afterward (1 Cor. 15:25–28)?

And who could assume this awesome responsibility other than those who are in Christ, who are called according to His purpose, and who are the salt of the earth and the light of the world? Christ defeated Satan at the cross, but it is His body, His people, who have been given the task of defeating Satan's forces on earth (Matt. 28:18–20; 2 Cor. 10:3–5).[27]

Historically, the Christian church held to an optimistic view of the future. Until a century or two ago, the general consensus was that the church would eventually conquer all forms of unbelief and would predominate throughout the world. This was most evident in English-speaking countries but was characteristic of the entire West earlier on. Hymns such as "Jesus shall reign where'er the sun shall his successive journeys run," and many others of similar vein gave evidence of the depth and extent of this faith. But the nineteenth century following the American and French revolutions, was a time of religious decline. The church grew feeble and was riddled with the rise of such cults as Mormonism, Russellism (Jehovah's Witnesses), Christian Science, and the like. In this weakened state, it was unable to satisfactorily answer the challenge of Darwinism and later grew pessimistic and either withdrew into itself (Pietism) or moved into the social gospel as their primary program.

In the case of Pietism, man's problem was seen to be himself, that is, his old nature that resides within his heart. The outside world was pushed back onto a very secondary back burner since the real enemy to be fought was the devil who has always been trying to deceive and cause us to fall into sin. So to be a true Christian was to achieve a state of being in which the devil's temptations were totally resisted. This inwardly directed focus left little or no concern for what was going on in the

---

27 For further study of Christian Reconstruction, see: R. J. Rushdoony, *Roots of Christian Reconstruction.* Vallecito, CA: Ross House Books, 1991); and R. J. Rushdoony, *Salvation and Godly Rule.* Vallecito, CA: Ross House Books, 1983.

external world, and as a result the church largely abandoned the culture.

In the second case, the social gospel (the path of most mainline churches), the church pulled back from its Christian roots and redirected the Christian emphasis to focus particularly on caring for the poor and other social welfare programs. Eventually it merged with statist welfarism. In both cases, the church left the road to cultural domination wide-open to atheistic humanism.

Today, in response to the visible rise of humanistic power and the correspondingly weakened condition of Christianity, many English-speaking evangelical churches follow a system of Biblical interpretation known as Dispensationalism. J. N. Darby (an early member of the Brethren church in England) originated this teaching in the early nineteenth century. It puts Biblical history into a neat package, one that is easy to understand and explain but does not flow from Scripture alone. It requires a great deal of creative interpretation, which amounts to distortion.[28]

C. I. Scofield, a notorious individual,[29] picked up and popularized Dispensationalism. He embedded its tenets as notes within the "Scofield Reference Bible." This "Bible" contained, intermingled with the inspired words of Scripture, Scofield's own commentary. Contradictory as it was to the teaching of the churches of the day, it engendered considerable controversy. Nevertheless, much of the general public became enamored with it because they felt it gave them a better understanding of the meaning of Scripture. Many wanted their pastors to preach according to Scofield's notes and those that refused were replaced. It was a grass-roots revolution by an uneducated, Biblically illiterate church population that swept the new doctrines into the church.[30]

Today, Dallas Theological Seminary and a host of Bible schools and seminaries throughout the United States teach Dispensationalism.[31] It posits a God that changes the way He interacts with man during different

---

28 Joseph M. Canfield, *The Incredible Scofield and His Book*. Vallecito, CA: Ross House Books, 1988, 166–170.

29 http://poweredbychrist.homestead.com/files/cyrus/scofield.htm

30 Canfield, 166–170.

31 Canfield, 152. "Scofield was the head of the Southwestern School of the Bible in Dallas, forerunner of the Dallas Theological Seminary. That school, now located on Swiss Avenue, Dallas is a major center for the dissemination of Scofield's views."

dispensations of time. The current dispensation (since Christ) is called *Grace*. The previous dispensation (Moses to Christ) was called *Law*. Some modern Dispensationalists believe that the Jews will rebuild their Temple and resume animal sacrifices. They believe this to be true despite the clear teaching of Scripture that Christ is the final sacrifice and that the sacrifice of animals, which pointed to Christ, is now obsolete (see Heb. 9:23–28; 10:8–12).[32]

Its doctrine of eschatology (the study of end things) is extremely pessimistic: It declares that the world is so dominated by the devil that no matter what Christians do or how hard they try the world will grow more and more evil as the Last Days approach. Despite many failed predictions, most Dispensational theologians and pastors (and their congregations and media-program listeners) still believe the Last Days are near and that soon Christ will return and defeat the devil. Dispensational eschatology has been popularized by a great many books such as *The Late Great Planet Earth* by Hal Lindsey and more recently the *Left Behind* series by Tim LaHaye and Jerry B. Jenkins. These highly popular books, mostly novels, portray a world dominated by Satanic forces from which born-again, believing Christians are rescued in The Rapture while all unbelievers are left behind. It depicts a scene in which automobiles are wrecked and airplanes come crashing to the ground because their drivers and pilots are suddenly raptured away. All this is held to be predictable because it is falsely assumed to be an assured prophecy of God's word.

This pessimistic doctrine has effectively formalized a defeatist attitude toward the future by claiming that the Bible teaches that the church cannot and will not be victorious in this age (dispensation). Victory, they say, will only be realized when Christ returns to earth to establish His "millennial" kingdom. According to this doctrine, the church—the body of Christ—is not responsible for the current godless conditions. These conditions are the inevitable result of the unalterable working out of God's plan. The church's charter, they say, is limited to the proclamation of the Gospel message to "all the world" and the saving of souls along the way. Dispensationalism teaches that Satan holds legal title to the world and he will rule until Christ returns. This is a 180-degree reversal from

---

32 http://www.middletownbiblechurch.org/proph/templemi.htm.

the attitude that was prevalent for virtually the entire church age. This unscriptural doctrine has rendered the modern church impotent with regard to its ability to effectively combat the current trend away from a Christian and toward a humanistic world-order.

Because the Last Days scenario is presented and taken by many believers as God's truth, it has shifted the primary focus of Christian cultural activity from a long-term to a short-term emphasis. Consequently, Dispensational Christians turned from efforts to build God's kingdom on earth to "let's save the lost before it's too late" programs. They see the Lord's prayer petition "thy kingdom come" as being fulfilled at Christ's return but not beforehand. As a result of the subsequent substantial Christian withdrawal from the culture, the power of evil has risen dramatically; and this doctrine has then become, in essence, a self-fulfilling prophecy. Dispensationalists can now point to the rise of evil—which rise was abetted by their doctrine—as proof of their doctrine.

Sadly, even many of the Reformed churches have followed a similar path. While retaining sound doctrines generally and rejecting dispensational theology, they have dropped their previous optimistic view of the future[33] and are now also pessimistic. In their current view, defined as Amillennialism, there is no victory at all. The world will never be Christianized and only a remnant will be saved from an eternity in hell. As long as these doctrines continue to influence God's people into an attitude of resignation, God's charter to Adam and Eve—to be fruitful, to fill the earth with God-fearing, obedient people who worship God in spirit and in truth—will never be realized, and Christ, who crushed Satan's head and created a people unto Himself, may never be victorious in a global sense. He must be satisfied with only a very small fraction of the world's population, most of the world being eternally lost. This has led to the teaching that God's people cannot and should not attempt to apply God's word to the culture in any general sense. In this view, it is not meant so much as a guide for rulers and lawmakers as for spiritual and personal matters at the level of the individual or family.

This relegation of public affairs to non-Christians effectively implies

---

33 Iain H. Murray, *Jonathan Edwards: A New Biography*. Edinburgh, UK: The Banner of Truth Trust, 1987, 296 ff.

that unregenerate man is not entirely fallen but has retained the ability to rule himself without help from God in the natural world. Presumably he needs God for salvation and his personal affairs but not for society at large. This is false and a great departure from the Reformation teachings. Francis Schaeffer wrote of a mural by Paul Robert (1851–1923) on the courthouse wall in Lausanne that depicts the then current viewpoint that law stems from God's Word.[34] We see there a representation of Justice—without a blindfold—standing before an assembly of magistrates. She has her scales in one hand and a sword in the other pointing down toward a book entitled *The Law of God.* The idea is that Justice instructs the Judges from God's word, that it is His word that should undergird the laws of the nations. The Reformation has indeed deteriorated greatly since the days of Luther and Calvin.

There are many other theological deviations and deformations that have taken root in today's churches. But of all the problems found within Christianity, these theological deficiencies—the loss of God's law and the loss of a victorious view of the future—have done a great amount of damage to the Christian cause. Both were consequences that arose, not from the work of the enemy, but from within the church by church-recognized pastors, teachers, and theologians. This could have been averted by an informed laity, but sadly there has not been enough Scriptural understanding among church members to prevent these false beliefs from taking hold and becoming widespread.

---

34 *The Complete Works of Francis A. Schaeffer: A Christian Worldview,* Volume 5, "A Christian View of the West." Wheaton, IL: Crossway Books, 1985, 136.

9

PLURALISM

RELIGIOUS liberty has been the cry of oppressed people in every age. Its humanistic version has become the shibboleth verbalized ad nauseam in America and the Western world today. But what does it mean in a preponderantly Christian society? Should Christians permit Muslim mosques to be built wherever they please? Should they permit unbelievers to teach their children in the public schools? Where should the line be drawn? Pluralism—the idea that people of different religions can peaceably live together under a common law system—is unworkable. Law necessarily rests on religious faith, whether that faith is theistic or atheistic.

Where religious views differ, conflict arises and eventually one or another of the conflicting views wins out and governs as the law of the land. All others must acquiesce and either compromise or leave. The Pilgrims left England to avoid state-church imposed unbiblical practices. The early Christians also refused to compromise with the Roman Empire and suffered greatly for it but eventually won out and converted first Rome and then all of Europe to the Christian faith.

Faith and culture are irrevocably interdependent. They are essential complements that cannot continue to exist in conflict with each other. Faith informs the culture and the culture informs faith. That Christianity can continue to coexist through multiple generations in today's heathen cultural environment is doubtful. It must either protect itself from the debilitating influences of the surrounding culture and come to dominate it or, failing to do so, in time be subdued by it. Religious pluralism is never permanent, but is characteristic of a culture in transition from one faith to another.

This is the condition in America and most of the Western world today. Sadly, Christians in this nation and around the world do not appreciate this fact. They have bought into the idea that their faith is something solely between themselves and God. It is a private matter, they say, and hence there is no problem with other people having whatever faith they desire. They reason: "Their faith does not affect me or mine." But this is both wrong and foolish.

We can see from God's repeated injunctions to the nation of Israel to separate themselves from the surrounding nations how debilitating contact with heathen cultures is. The penalty for attempting to proselytize others to a false religion was severe: Israelites who did so were subject to the death penalty (see Deut. 13:6–9). That said, Christians should recognize that God did not establish any civil law prohibiting individuals from worshiping as they pleased. Anyone could worship any god he chose provided he didn't attempt to proselytize. Without entering into a discussion as to the differences between their society and ours, we can plainly see the importance that God places on the environment His people live in. He knows our frame, that we are but dust and are highly susceptible to the evil influences of false religions.

In a stable, steady-state condition, the culture supports the faith held by a population. Families can teach their faith to their children and expect them to grow up sharing the same values they themselves were taught a generation earlier. This is so because everyone (or almost everyone) they come into contact with supports that same faith. They re-enforce rather than oppose and conflict with each other. Young people grow up, not ignorant of alternative faiths, but understanding them in a proper light with an appreciation of their many deficiencies and a knowledge of why they believe what they believe.

Many supporters of pluralism argue that the early Christians lived and thrived in a pluralistic society. What they fail to consider, though, is that wherever the true faith is suppressed and forced underground, it forms a culture around itself that is basically Christian. It is then able to survive and even grow in size, strength, and influence. The pockets of Christianity formed by Paul and the other apostles were strong enough in the faith to resist attempts to integrate them into the surrounding pagan culture. They maintained their own subculture which, the Lord enabling them, eventually coalesced into a force that took over the whole of the European continent.

For more than a thousand years, Europe was known as "Christendom." The vast majority of the population recognized Christ as the ultimate ruler whose word was the final authority above that of whoever might be on the throne at the time. The will of the majority, if not their own conviction, forced kings to acknowledge Christ as Lord and Master and submit to His will. The Europe of the Middle Ages was decidedly not a pluralistic society. This is not to say there were no exceptions or that obedience was total. It certainly was not. Sin was as present then as it is today and corruption became so prevalent that the upheaval of the Reformation became unavoidable. It does show, however, the strength inherent in God's providence working through the Christian faith to conquer and maintain dominion over cultures at the national level.

In places like China and portions of Africa such as Southern Sudan where Christianity is undergoing significant persecution, it is growing in depth as well as breadth. One major contributing factor to this growth is the uniformity of the faith throughout the families isolated and united by the persecution. Others of like faith surround each individual and the youth especially are not confused with differing religious views. These groups, like the early churches, effectively form their own cultures and become relatively impervious to potentially damaging external influence. The same is true of emigrants from Muslim countries today, particularly in Europe. They bring with them their own customs, mosques, schools, and even their laws and remain isolated from the post-Christian cultures of the European countries they emigrate to. They are not really immigrants; they are colonists establishing outposts of their faith in these countries.

In the pluralistic society that we see around us today, families that wish to pass their faith to their children are compromised by their inability to isolate them from the irreligious ideas of individuals or groups they come into contact with. Many mature, doctrinally orthodox Christian parents are sorrowing over wayward children and grandchildren. They feel they have done a reasonably good job of raising them and don't understand why they have left the faith. Parents can do an excellent job and yet have it be subverted by a trusted friend or schoolteacher or anyone the child comes into contact with who impresses him or her favorably. Sports figures, TV personalities, books, movies, popular music, and social media exert a cumulative effect on the mind of the growing, learning child or youth. To think that the cultural impact on the faith is negligible or easily compensated for is extremely foolish. It is a highly charged and relentless propaganda that drives home the message that there is no God. Perhaps the most insidious form this takes is simply the omission of any reference to God throughout a book or movie or during the whole day at school. The silence is effectively a loud declaration of the non-existence of God.

To think that our faith or that of our children is so strong as to remain unaffected by a repeated barrage of this kind of material is to play the ostrich and hide one's head in the sand. The Pilgrims had this problem in Holland where, although they were welcome and well-treated, they saw the effect the ungodly environment was having on their youth and felt they needed to leave, even though they knew a terrible cost would be involved. They had more understanding of the seriousness of the problem than we see among Christians in our day who have attempted to continue to practice their faith in an increasingly antagonistic culture. This is more the case among Dispensationalists who have relegated the world to Satan, but it is also sadly true of the Reformed churches as well. Many of the latter claim to hold to a world and life view of the faith but really limit it to self, family, and church. Neither group makes any sort of serious attempt to change the culture. Apart from the current abortion controversy where some resistance is being offered, the outside world does not seem to feel any serious challenge from most Christians. God's name is rarely brought into the public square. Instead of citing God's word, Christians merely assert their opinion versus other opinions on any subject under debate. Even in the arguments brought against abortion, instead of "thus saith the Lord," we hear arguments about the danger to the mother, the psychological trauma, etc., usually accompanied by insipid pleas for some sort of compromise position. To invoke God's law as the basis for opposition to abortion or anything else has become almost unthinkable. This exemplifies the extremes to which the acceptance of religious pluralism has driven Christianity. Christians have bought into the concept of a pluralism-tolerant and open society. They are largely oblivious to the fact that they are losing the war, and the world is leading them, like sheep, to the slaughter.

10

Humanism

THE struggle for religious control in America is primarily between Christianity and humanism. Humanism in the West takes its modern, narrow form; it denies the existence of any god and sees mankind as its own god. It denies creation and goes to Darwinistic evolution and the Big Bang to explain origins. There is, though, considerable variation among humanists. Some, wearing sheep's clothing, affirm belief in God and may even go to church, but they don't see God as Creator and Lawgiver, that is, as Lord of their lives. They see Him rather as a resource they can employ to their own ends. Such persons make themselves gods of their own lives and therefore are, by definition, humanists. They may be counted as believers by some, but they have not made the transition to the Christian faith. This dilution of Christianity is a significant factor in its decline.

Humanists have successfully employed the concept of religious pluralism as a ploy to effect a transition from Christianity to their form of faith. They first—playing on the idea of religious liberty, which to Christians means freedom to worship the true God in the Christian denomination of one's choice—expanded it to mean the freedom to worship any god one chooses. They then took this view into the political realm through the argument that laws should represent all religions, or, at least, that laws should not offend anyone's faith or lack thereof.

This, carried to the extreme, is where we stand today: law must remain religiously neutral—an impossible condition. Law is never religiously neutral, but is intrinsically religious in that law is rooted in morality, morality is rooted in ultimacy and values, and ultimacy and values are religious concepts. Law is an enactment of the beliefs of one religion or another. Where the concepts of humanism conflicted with those of Christianity, the latter are being, one by one, displaced by the former. This transition, championed by the American Civil Liberties Union (ACLU), has been especially rapid since World War II. The ACLU has been highly effective in using the media and the courts to cause a steady transfer of our laws from a Christian to a humanistic basis. We now have a situation where— despite an alleged Christian population of 80% or more—it is primarily humanistic thought that dictates law in America.

Today's secular public school system is openly anti-Christian: no Bibles are permitted, and no mention of God, Christ, or anything related to the Christian religion is tolerated. The public school system has been and still is a powerful engine of indoctrination of America's youth. Its primary purpose is not, as they would have you believe, to provide a general education; it is to lead the youth of America away from Christianity—from moral, family, and also American Christian values they learn at home—and to indoctrinate them into humanistic beliefs. It is an insidious establishment of the religion of humanism, exactly what is denied to Congress by the First Amendment.

Christians could have prevented all of this from taking place, but due to their lack of understanding and lack of concern they just stood apathetically on the sidelines and watched it happen. This is still very much the case today. If Christians would vote as a block, they would carry most every election in a landslide. Instead what we see is that typically 50% of the Christian community doesn't even register to vote and those who do fail to vote for the candidates or parties that offer a reasonably Christian platform. Instead, because of their short-term focus, they vote for the candidates they see as being the lesser of two evils. Since the lesser evil is still evil, humanism continues to grow and gains more power and influence every year.

The late Dr. D. James Kennedy, founder of Coral Ridge Church and Ministries (now Truth In Action Ministries) in Ft. Lauderdale, FL, in his lifelong battle to reverse this kind of ostrich-like behavior, quoting Dr. Don Wildmon, founder of American Family Association in Tupelo, MS, repeated several times in one of his sermons that despite the many flagrant anti-Christian laws that were being proposed and enacted, 300,000 pulpits remained silent. Dr. Kennedy was almost a lone voice in the wilderness crying out to Christians to awaken them to the great need to get involved in politics to combat the cultural changes that were taking place with such great rapidity. Dr. Kennedy may have not fully recognized the extent to which this over-arching silence in the pulpits was a consequence of the theology held by the occupants of those pulpits. He did a good deal of great work in addressing and alerting Christians as to what was wrong and what needed to be done, but he didn't attempt to uncover and expose the theological foundations of the problem. Dr. R. J. Rushdoony, the late founder of Chalcedon Foundation, Vallecito, CA, went a step further in uncovering and exposing the roots of the problem, in a very thorough and comprehensive manner.[35] However, most church leaders have not welcomed his message. It was too different from what they had been taught in Bible school or seminary; they preferred to remain inert and content with the status quo. So humanism continues its march toward total cultural domination.

Christians, understandably, have become discouraged by the rise of humanism in the culture. But few seem to realize that, had Christians been fully obedient to God and exercised the dominion implied in His command to be salt and light, this would never have taken place. Pastors and theologians (both Amillennial and Premillennial) then, in what appears almost like a coverup for failure, redefined eschatology to say that victory could only be realized after Christ's physical return and that the world would become progressively worse until then. Also, many theologians and Christian leaders are convincing themselves and a large segment of the church that Christ's return is imminent. This kind of thinking has led to a critical withdrawal of Christians from public affairs. Acting on what they believed to be God's truth, they have lost interest—or at least long-term interest—in this world and turned their focus away from worldly affairs toward preparation for heaven and the afterlife.

Evangelism continues but not in the same form as earlier. It has become an attempt to get as many people as possible saved before the Lord's return. This new theological perspective grows rapidly as it initiates a snowballing effect wherein, as Christians withdraw from society, humanists are better able to undermine the established order. As they

---

35 For more on the works of Rushdoony, see: www.chalcedon.edu.

see evil increasing, more and more Christians are drawn into this new theology. They in turn relinquish their responsibility to society, and the movement continues to grow. Today, it appears that most of the body of Christ, the true believers, are members of churches that subscribe to this or similar pessimistic views of eschatology.

This is precisely what Christ warned against when He said, "Ye are the salt of the earth: but if the salt have lost his savour, wherewith shall it be salted? It is thenceforth good for nothing, but to be cast out, and to be trodden under foot of men" (Matt. 5:13).

Christianity is being trodden under the foot of humanism because its salt has lost its savor. All this has transpired because Christians have disobeyed God and God has withdrawn His hand of blessing and is now chastising His people. We could say that we are suffering from the logical consequences of our actions, or lack thereof, and that is true. But God is still in control and until obedience is restored His chastisement will continue.

PART THREE

THE
WAY
FORWARD

11

CONSIDERATIONS

CHRISTIANITY has strayed so far from its moorings that what we might consider a move forward, most people—even many of today's Christians—would probably consider a move backward. Standing where we are today and considering the relative numbers of people on each side of the issue, the task of reestablishing godly rule on any scale would seem monumental, if not utterly impossible. Its supporters would seem to be out of their minds and in need of psychiatric therapy, but that is far from the truth of the matter. The reality is that humanism is now in the later stages of decay. It cannot survive if it continues on its current path—but, just as the leopard cannot change its spots, humanism also cannot change its path. The only political alternatives for man are godly rule or a dog-eat-dog world that vacillates between totalitarianism and anarchy. As more people, especially Christians, become aware of this reality, what is now a tiny movement in support of godly rule will grow to become a tidal wave that will inundate the opposition. Do not despise the potential of small beginnings (1 Sam. 14:6; Zech. 4:10). Believe God and obey Him, and He will right all wrongs.

We've slid so far down that the way of progress is, in one sense, indeed a move backward. We need to go back and regain the ground that has been lost—but that alone is not sufficient. To go back and then follow the same steps we took before would just put us right back into the mess we now have. But, in fact, because today's Christians do not have the same foundation the early church had, the result might be even worse. If we are to move ahead without repeating the mistakes of the past, there are many factors that need to be taken into consideration and some serious changes required in Christian practice.

The following is not intended as anywhere near a complete list or even a list of the most important areas. Rather, it represents this author's opinion of some of the places where many churches and Christian institutions have gone astray.

OBEYING GOD

The key to cultural recovery for Christians is total obedience to God's law. In principle, it's really as simple as that. If Christians would begin to obey God's word in every respect, without reservations or qualifications, God has promised showers of blessings (see Ezek. 34:22–31). This obedience though, must be total; it cannot be edited or restricted either willfully or in ignorance. As we noted earlier, James clearly showed us that to willfully reject any of God's laws is to reject them all. Due to the sin nature that is present in all of us, even professing Christians may do this at times, but such an attitude, if not followed by repentance, demonstrates a lack of true faith.

Largely through ignorance, Christians have failed to obey many of God's laws and actually have never obeyed all His laws at any point in history. Whether we fail to obey out of ignorance or because we have been misled, we are still culpable. Knowledge of God's Word then, is important. Scripture is replete with passages extolling the virtues of and the need for knowledge:

> My people are destroyed for lack of knowledge: because thou hast rejected knowledge, I will also reject thee. (Hos. 4:6)

> The fear of the LORD is the beginning of knowledge: but fools despise wisdom and instruction. (Prov. 1:7)

> How long, ye simple ones, will ye love simplicity? and the scorners delight in their scorning, and fools hate knowledge? (Prov. 1:22)

> Where there is no vision, the people perish: but he that keepeth the law, happy is he. (Prov. 29:18)

> Give me now wisdom and knowledge, that I may go out
> and come in before this people: for who can judge this thy
> people, that is so great? (2 Chr. 1:10)

Hosea 4:6 tells us that destruction is the consequence of a lack of knowledge and a nation that rejects knowledge invokes God's rejection. Without a vision, the people perish (Pr. 29:18). We ignore these injunctions to our own detriment. Christians need to study and become familiar with God's word if the faith is to make progress in this world.

It is important that knowledge of the faith be widely distributed and not reserved to a few. There will always be differences in the amount of knowledge individuals have, but every Christian should strive to understand for himself the meaning of Scripture. Without this level of attention to the word by all believers, false doctrines enter into the church and eventually so distort the truth that it can become the opposite of what is intended therein. An uninformed laity is easily swayed by devious arguments, arguments that sound good on the surface but internally are contradictory to Scripture. It is not enough to rely on "good theologians" to combat this tendency. We do need theologians to help us in our efforts to understand Scripture, but even the best of them cannot, in the absence of an informed laity, restrain the dissemination and eventual acceptance of false theology, theology that leads to disobedience. It is only a Biblically astute and concerned laity, one that can discern and identify false theology, that can guard against the distortion or damage which could result from false teaching and false teachers.

In Matthew 6:33, after a long dissertation on the foolishness of worry about the necessities of life, Christ said, "But seek ye first the kingdom of God, and His righteousness; and all these things shall be added unto you." He places here two things that are to be sought after, even before our natural concerns for food, clothing, and shelter. To seek the kingdom of God is to work to effect His kingdom in one's own life *and* in the world outside. Since a kingdom is the domain in which the word of the king is law, we have here yet another admonition for Christians to be about establishing God's word as the law of the land where they live. To seek God's righteousness is to work to apply His law in every situation where we have responsibility or influence. This is not a difficult passage to understand, but it is often spiritualized away by teachers who—most often through lack of proper understanding—hinder God's work in this world. The churches are sorely in need of knowledgeable Christians who are diligent to question and correct all teachings that lead away from the truth of God's word.

God's moral laws are really not very different from His physical laws. One cannot ignore the law of gravity without potentially incurring damage to his person. One cannot consume poisonous substances without experiencing detrimental physiological effects. When God's laws regarding cleanliness and hygiene are ignored, even in an otherwise godly society, disease and pestilence follow. Likewise, when a people fail to love their neighbors, societal ills and criminal activity ensue over time.

God promises that blessings will flow from obedience. This is commonly taken as being a gift from His hand, a reward He bestows upon His obedient child. While there is truth in this view, it is also true that obedience to God's commandments often contains within itself the blessing. This is especially true with respect to an obedient culture or society. Love your neighbor returns a myriad of blessings to everyone in a godly society. Everyone benefits when the preponderant majority obeys God's laws. Obedience in this sense, however imperfect, was the engine of growth that developed the Christian West.

Obedience sometimes means struggle and sacrifice. When Moses sat on a hill overlooking the battle between Israel and Amalek, it was Joshua and the Israelites that were fighting and dying in the battle below (see Exod. 17:8–12). God gave victory while Moses held up his staff, but it was still the responsibility of the Israelites to fight the enemy—to deal mortal blows and to suffer and die from wounds inflicted upon them. David spent many years in hiding and fighting for his life before he was finally made king. Likewise, we need to realize that the world will not be made Christian without the sacrifices and sufferings of battles fought on our part. We will not be brought to heaven on flowery beds of comfort and ease. Christ did not give us a superficial task; it is one that will require real and sometimes painful effort to complete. We are promised though that the reward will outshine and eclipse all the difficulties we experience.

Obedience to God's civil laws, the laws that require civil penalties, must also be observed. While these cannot be instituted until Christian influence is sufficiently great and the people as a whole are ready for it, it must be made a part of the visible agenda from the first and not be hidden. Christians especially, but unbelievers as well, need to be educated as to the need for and the blessings to be derived from these laws.

Total obedience then is what is required of us though this does not mean *perfect* obedience. Since Christ's ascension, perfection is not to be found on earth; we are all still bearers of the sin nature Adam infected us with and nothing we do is ever perfect. What is needed though is an attitude of submission to God's word wherein we diligently attempt to obey Him instead of judging Him by ideas extraneous to His word.

We read in 2 Chronicles 7:14: "If my people, which are called by my name, shall humble themselves, and pray, and seek my face, and turn from their wicked ways; then will I hear from heaven, and will forgive their sin, and will heal their land."

These words are a call for revival, not among unbelievers but among those who take Christ's name and call themselves Christians. Their land is sick and needs healing because they lack humility and walk in wicked ways. They have turned their backs on God and live in disobedience to His law. But God says He will have mercy and forgive them if they will return to Him and pray as His obedient creatures. This promise was given thousands of years ago but God does not go back on His word and it is still true today. As we begin to obey, truly and totally obey Him, the healing process will commence.

POLITICS

This country was transitioned from a republic into a democracy as a consequence of events surrounding the Civil War, and culminating in the Wilson Administration with the income tax, the Federal Reserve, and the direct election of senators. But because democracies can be inherently unstable, it has now, for all practical purposes, degenerated into an oligarchy—rule by the few. Lincoln paraphrased the words generally attributed to John Wycliffe: "This Bible is for the government of the people, by the people, and for the people." [36] It retains in form a government of

---

36 John Wycliffe, General Prologue of the *Wycliffe Translation of the Bible*, 1384. As quoted by Rousas Rushdoony in *The Institutes of Biblical Law*, The Presbyterian and Reformed Publishing Company, 1973, 1. Also paraphrased in speeches by Daniel Webster, 1830; Theodore Parker, 1850; and Abraham Lincoln, Gettysburg Address, 1863.

the people but it is by and for the wealthy and powerful. What took place with the TARP legislation of 2008 should be ample proof. An overwhelming majority of Americans were against that legislation but Congress ignored the will of the people and cast democracy aside. This is not a unique event; our leaders have repeatedly set aside public opinion to act in their own interests.

Today we have presidents, congressional representatives, judges, and officials at every level of government whose only interests are reelection, maintenance or advancement of their positions, the wealth they can accumulate, and the power they can wield. Many do not have the slightest interest in the well-being of their constituents and are quite ready to flush them down the drain if need be to further their own selfish ends. These men, whether elected or appointed, are controlled by a small number of very rich and very powerful individuals that comprise what amounts to an oligarchy. The American system was designed to eliminate or at least minimize here the power that the aristocracy wielded in Europe. But today this principle has degenerated to the point that not only is there an aristocracy in America, but because a very small number of multi-billionaires really control things, it is better described as an oligarchy. It is not wealth that is the problem; it is that great power elicits from fallen men the temptation to act as gods. As Lord Acton said, "power tends to corrupt and absolute power corrupts absolutely."[37] While we recognize no absolute power on earth, we can see the danger associated with aggregating extremely great power into the hands of a few, known or unknown.

America goes through the motions of operating as a democratic society and the pretense of being a representative republic that functions according to its constitution; but, in reality, for all practical purposes, the outcomes of elections are determined, not by the general public but by the oligarchy. Its control is effectuated by means of their control of the information media, schools and universities, labor and industry, and the elected individuals who owe their offices to the large contributions they have been given. This oligarchy is not monolithic; there are the more radical and more moderate constituents. It is largely comprised of atheistic

---

37 http://www.bartleby.com/cgi-bin/texis/webinator/sitesearch?FILTER=colQuotations &query=power+tends+to+corrupt+and+absolute+power+corrupts+absolutely

humanists, ostensibly irreligious, but, in fact, are very *"religiously"* intent on aggrandizing greater and greater power to themselves and to the total elimination of the Christian faith. In this regard, they reflect as well as lead the culture toward a more and more consistent humanistic faith. Some might object to the use of the term "oligarchy" (rule by a few) to describe this element; but through their ability to shape public thinking, these often hidden (unelected) insiders do effectively rule the nation.

Now, many would say that this is conspiracy theory in the extreme, but that is not the case. While there is no doubt a degree of cooperation between like-minded individuals, it is not so much concerted effort as merely the religious outworking of their beliefs, which are rooted in their fundamental sinful nature, that we see in action. These individuals are not secretly plotting to overthrow law and order; they are doing what they believe ought to be done. They are applying the principles of their philosophy and faith to the culture. (Christians should have this kind of dedication to their beliefs.) As graduates of the finest universities and members of the best clubs and fraternities, these individuals are well-versed and highly consistent humanistic thinkers. Most were born into wealthy families and have been brought up to see themselves as the natural leaders of society. They are not so much interested in accumulating more wealth as in what they see as improving society. For some, this amounts to educating the lower classes to the supposed merits of their atheistic blind-faith beliefs. For others, their goal is increased power over the lives of the common people so they can be compelled, against their will, into becoming the kind of society they believe is best for all. For both, the long-term goal is to do away with the Christian faith, which they see as a major impediment to the advancement of society, to their idea of the next level of development. In general, they see themselves as builders, not destroyers, magnanimous contributors to the betterment of society. They apply the power that comes with great wealth to accomplish these purposes, purposes that derive from their humanistic faith. Satan does not directly control them, as some believe; they are gods unto themselves—they have adopted the faith of fallen Adam and Eve and are living it out consistently.

All this apparent altruism, though, is a surface phenomenon. As God's word tells us, these paragons of society are actually in rebellion against the true God. They know that God is their Creator but they are suppressing that knowledge in unrighteousness (see Rom. 1:18–21). They abhor and reject the thought of a God in heaven, a God that has laid down a law *they* are bound to obey and by which *they* will eventually be judged. They represent the upper echelons of the seed of the serpent and their efforts need to be resisted with all the means God allows us.

The above is a sad commentary on the conditions that prevail in governments throughout the world today and in America in particular. We need to thoroughly understand that this has come about as a consequence of the failure of American leaders after the founding era to carry out God's commandments with respect to civil government. Into the nineteenth century Americans began to foolishly neglect God's laws in their stewardship of the institutions they received. They became lax in regard to the outworking of the sin nature that resides in every child of Adam. The founders had declared that America's elected officials ought to be Christians, but did not make it a legal requirement in the Constitution. Later Americans failed to produce and forward Christian statesmen. While Christians sat on their hands in their pews, Americans allowed socialistic so-called progressives to work into the fabric of our government counter-Biblical and counter-constitutional policies. Instead of retaining familial control of education, they instituted government-run public schools that have deteriorated into engines of atheistic propaganda. They permitted other religions and their evils the protections of liberty, due only to Biblical faith, and to proselytize without restraint. In many other respects they ignored God's law, and today we see the fruits of their disobedience in the moral character of both our nation's leaders and our nation as a whole.

Given the above, we can see that the transition to a godly society cannot be effected through the state or through political action or through revolution. It is the moral character of the nation that decides the kind of government by which the nation is ruled. Also, as George Washington warned us in 1796, "let us with caution indulge the supposition that morality can be maintained without religion." Contrary to humanistic creed, human nature is not basically good; it is fallen and tends always to evil: "there is none that doeth good, no, not one" (see Rom. 3:12). Morality is informed and shaped by its religious roots. Political action is necessary but, of necessity, it cannot lead but must follow; it can only proceed to the extent to which the necessary moral base has first been established. It is truly said, "people get the government they deserve." An immoral people will not elect moral leaders and will not get good government.

It is only the regenerating power of the Holy Spirit working in the hearts of men that will accomplish God's purposes in America and throughout the world. It will be a grassroots movement that needs no organization, no mass meetings, no massive marketing programs, no political parties, no war chests, nor any of the usual means customarily employed to effect social change. It must not and will not employ physical force in any form to institute the changes it advocates. Christians cannot attempt to *impose* their views of religion or morality on others.

The power that advances the faith is truth. Truth brings understanding and understanding, wisdom. The fool says in his heart there is no God and thinks in his foolishness that he can do anything he desires; but a wise person recognizes his own limitations: that he is God's creature and is dependent upon his Creator for both life and direction in life. As people begin to understand that they must look to God for political direction and that any other approach to government always leads to failure, they will see the utter fallacy of attempting to govern themselves without God and God's word. The fact that we have a word from God—that He has not been silent but has spoken to us—is one of mankind's greatest blessings. Our greatest curse is that we have not paid attention to the ultimate wisdom found therein, but have played the fool to our own destruction.

Christians need to stop selling Jesus merely as a way to peace in this life and bliss in the next. They also need to focus on the dire need for God in everyday life and in every institution of man, including civil government. When they do so in sufficient numbers, the world will begin to sit up and take notice. The opposition will become more bitter and vehement in their attacks, but the irresistible force of truth will eventually prevail and many unbelievers will listen and be converted.

As more and more Christians begin to truly obey God's law in their own lives and in their interaction with the world, they will encourage others to do the same and God will cause their numbers and their influence in society at large to increase commensurately. Concurrent with this growth, civil law will begin to shift away from the humanistic character it now has and begin to take on a more Christian character. Eventually we will see predominantly Christian societies governed by Christians and operating under God's law.

This obviously cannot be done in a day and the transition will more likely be measured in generations rather than years. To expedite progress Christians must take the long view in the situations they face and resist the temptation to take what seem to be shortcuts but actually represent compromise that most often results in delay, or worse, regress. When they do, we will see real progress begin and the end result will be the fulfillment of the Great Commission of Christ, a truly Christian world.

CHURCH AND FAMILY

In Scripture, the family is central to society. It is the primary institution. The family was instituted prior to the Fall (Genesis 1:28, 2:22–25), while the church and civil government are secondary, having been added as a consequence of the Fall and sin. Society was viewed to consist of families, not individuals or organizations as it generally is today. Much of God's word is devoted to how families should function both internally and externally. Much of God's law refers to relationships within the family. Three of the Ten Commandments speak directly to the family: the fifth, seventh, and tenth (Exo. 20:12, 14, 17).

To appreciate the importance God assigns to family, we need to be aware of the extent to which family is involved in the societal structure God gives us in His word. The whole of society to the highest levels is based on family. The nation of Israel was composed of tribes; family rather than geographic commonality pervaded the entire concept of government. Heads of state were not elected officials representing residents of their regional districts; to the extent they existed, they were tribal leaders. This is not very visible because, prior to the monarchy, the central government was of miniscule size and significance. Due to the current faith in big government that has been promoted by pseudo-intellectuals who dominate our colleges and universities, tribalism is viewed today as a primitive and outmoded form of government. But it is the structure God put in place in ancient Israel, and we can see that His wisdom is reflected in that choice as it is in all things. Political units that are family oriented would tend to be much more tightly integrated than geographically determined bodies and, hence, more difficult to subjugate by larger bodies. Tribalism as it existed in ancient Israel would probably not fit directly into the modern situation, but the principles embodied therein should not be discarded out-of-hand. Tribal civil government may not be the solution for today's society, but godly, restrained, local self-government is certainly a step in the right direction.

Humanism is anti-family: It gives lip service to the God-ordained authority of family but refuses to submit to God in this area or in anything else. It sees the family as an impediment to the continual increase of state power and opposes it at every turn. The promotion of feminism, homosexuality, and pornography are just the most obvious of many humanistic attempts to undermine the Biblical family. The strength and power of the family has been seriously compromised over the last few decades by these efforts—but it has not been defeated. Family is so intricately intertwined with human nature and God's order that much of its vigor still remains. The battle lines are clearly drawn and Christians are in the forefront. If they recognize what is at stake and actively participate in the struggle, victory is assured.

The Nuclear Family

The godly family consists of father, mother, and children living harmoniously together under God's law. This means that the husband is the head of the wife, that the husband is to love his wife as Christ loved the church and gave Himself for it, and that children are to obey their parents (see Eph. 5:21–6:3). This God-given structure is under heavy attack today. As an institution, its influence in society has been reduced. It is now less able to interpose itself between the members of the family unit and that growing behemoth, the humanistic state. The state's power over individuals grows as these intermediate levels of government—the family, the church, and other associations—are weakened.

The weakening of the family structure has progressed to the degree that today most marriage vows no longer include the wife's promise to obey her husband. The result of this is that unity in the modern family (even in the churches) is increasingly disrupted, and the authority of the family, both internally and externally, is greatly weakened.

Many Christians argue that in some families the wife is clearly the superior of her husband and therefore should be the leader. While the premise here is certainly true, the conclusion is problematical. Here again we are faced with the question: Do we obey God or, because this is a sensitive subject that represents a major deviation from modern thinking, do we revert to our own feelings, intuitions, and reasoning for direction? Does this mean that God was wrong when He stated in Ephesians 5:

23 For the husband is the head of the wife, even as Christ is the head of the church: and he is the saviour of the body.

24 Therefore as the church is subject unto Christ, so let the wives be to their own husbands in every thing.

Are we wiser than God? If so, we don't need His word and we can no longer call ourselves Christians. We will have become humanists and have no need of God or His word. The word of God is not like a smorgasbord from which we can pick and choose that which is pleasing to our appetites and reject the rest. Whether we reject it outright, or if through devious means of interpretation we circumvent the intent of the plain text, is immaterial. It is the command-word of the Creator to His creatures, the basis on which He will judge the world that we are trifling with. We disdain to obey at our peril.

A wise and godly wife who finds herself in such a circumstance can still have a great deal of influence in her family affairs but not by asserting her will over her husband's. She should honor and obey God by recognizing her husband's God-given authority and not violate it. Even when she feels that he is about to make a mistake, she should not go beyond persuasion in her attempts to correct him. A truly wise wife would be more concerned about obedience to God than accomplishing her own desires through disobedience. The wife, if she believes that her husband is about to violate God's Law-Word, is morally responsible to not abet or participate in his sin. The husband's authority is limited: It is authority under God. God's commands supersede his own. He may not require what God forbids or forbid what God commands. Both within and without the family, all Christians (women as well as men) must obey God rather than men. When human authority is in conflict with God's Law-Word, it is God that must be obeyed.

This formula—husbands love your wives and wives submit yourselves to your husbands—is the backbone of the Biblical family. It is the God-given means to a healthy, productive, peaceful, and happy way of life. Let's not throw it away for something that may seem to be better but in the long run will prove to be far worse.

Because the family is now in an extremely debilitated state, the Biblical concept of family as the basic and controlling level of society may seem far-fetched and unrealistic in today's world. But it is God's way, the way God has ordained for the structure of society. Individualism, misunderstood and misapplied within the family has often disintegrated the nuclear family into separate, virtually disconnected, atomistic individuals. It has been carried to the point that in some states children can now bring suit against their parents for the crime of mental cruelty, to say nothing of corporal punishment. Much effort will be needed to undo the many structures that have been erected to undermine the family and erode its influence in society.

But even long before all this began, the concept of the extended family was already greatly diluted.

The Extended Family

The strength of the family lies, not so much in the nuclear family, as in the unity of the extended family. As in cultures and governments throughout history, it has always been the strength of the intermediate levels that has resisted or prevented the upper power structures, often controlled by a power-seeking few, from exploiting and enslaving relatively defenseless individuals.

God instituted the family in a hierarchical structure with Adam as the original family head. He, with Eve as his helper, was charged with the Dominion Mandate, to populate and establish a God-fearing, Christian world (Gen. 1:26–27). Each successive generation was to have been under the authority of the previous one. We see that structure carried through in ancient Israel, wherein the twelve tribes are seen to be a succession of families as God commanded (see Numbers chapters 1–4, and Joshua 13:15–31).

The extended family, knit together through blood ties, forms the lowest and most important level of protection from the power-hungry elite that desire to exercise direct control over individuals. When families virtually break up and often scatter as the youth marry or divorces occur, the effectiveness of the extended family is materially reduced. The power of this group of now relatively disconnected families is only a fraction of what it would be had it been held together as a solid unit. Immature individuals in their twenties or thirties are now making decisions with limited leadership, support, or advice from their elders. Worse yet, they are unable to coordinate their efforts and are often manipulated and led by outside influences. The older generation, that has the experience and wisdom the younger lacks, loses its authority and much of its influence and is pushed into the background, relegated to baby-sitting and similar innocuous activities.

The success of the Great Commission, a restatement of the Dominion Mandate, depends heavily on the strength of the extended family. When we consider just one aspect—the fact that the family is a potential producer of compounded wealth—we can see how powerful it could become and why the ruling elite are constantly at war with them, diligently working to break them up and keep them in subjugation. This wealth, recognized as belonging to God with the family as steward, growing as it is handed down from generation to generation and employed in the building of God's kingdom, will eventually provide the financial means through which the Great Commission will be fulfilled.

Our own, as well as the cultures of the rest of the world must be brought into subjection to the King of kings and made His footstool. This is indeed a tall order but God is faithful and has given us the means to carry it out. The family in this Biblical sense is a key factor in the equation.

Education

Concerning the training of children, it is important to understand that faith must be inculcated and not left to the choice of the young. If we believe that God has spoken in His word and that word is truth, we must do all we can to insure that our faith is propagated. We must not leave open any doors through which seeds of doubt can enter and confuse the young and yet unlearned. As they grow in the knowledge of the truth, the question of why one believes can and should be addressed and discussed with greater and greater freedom. They will face this as their exposure increases with age and they need to be well-versed in God's word and have a good comprehension of the reason and foundation for their faith. We read in Deuteronomy 6:

> 6 And these words, which I command thee this day, shall be in thine heart:

> 7 And thou shalt teach them diligently unto thy children, and shalt talk of them when thou sittest in thine house, and when thou walkest by the way, and when thou liest down, and when thou risest up.

God instructs us here to keep His words in our heart; they are to be vitally important to us, central to how we live our lives, something to think about often. We are to explain them to our children at every opportunity so that they will develop the same understanding and concern for their further propagation. The faith should not die out in a generation. Rather, as families obey this injunction, both faith and understanding should grow over time.

This kind of training in the faith cannot be left to schools and teachers, not even Christian schools. It must be done at home, and father as well as mother must participate. Children must see the faith of their parents, especially that of the father. They must see a real and deeply held faith that is based on both God's word and reason, not just a blind faith that is held to without any understanding of why it is believed. Only then will they grow up into strong believers and supporters of the faith themselves. Only then will they possess the wherewithal to resist and do battle with the forces of evil they will eventually come into contact with.

Many well-meaning Christians have not taken this approach. They don't understand why their children reject the faith they were exposed to in their early years. They underestimate the pernicious effect even a relatively small exposure to humanistic thinking can have on their children. They see their children as basically good and forget that the old nature resides in them. Through ignorance or neglect they fail to obey God's commandment to "bring them up in the nurture and admonition of the Lord" (see Eph. 6:4), and the damage is done.

For this reason alone we can see that education must be a family responsibility. It cannot be left to the state, especially a humanistic state that will undermine the faith of the youth. None of us are born with the ability to love as God commands us to love; it can only be developed through discipline and training. When teaching our youth, we can't procrastinate beyond the early years without pain to both the individual and society as a whole. Here again we see the kinds of consequences that follow from a failure to fully obey God's commandments.

The Church

What is the proper role of the church? As God commanded, it is to be, as the household of "the living God, the pillar and ground of the truth" (see 1 Tim. 3:15). Its work is to support God's word through first studying to understand it rightly and then proclaiming and teaching it. It should exposit and clearly convey the meaning of God's instructions regarding the responsibilities of Christian individuals, families, and other institutions. This is not a trivial task and cannot be accomplished successfully without full dedication and firm resistance to sidetracks into non-Biblical activities.

The church as an institution is patterned after the synagogue model (not the Temple) where ten or more family heads formed a local worshipping body. These family heads, in accordance with the teachings of Scripture, governed and supported all the activities of this body including discipline, order of worship, and the election of officers from their number. Those capable of teaching were given opportunity to do so at the behest of these family heads. They formed the congregation, which (as in some churches even today) was measured in terms of families rather than individuals. Wives and children, widows, etc. were members of families and congregation members in a less direct sense. Church officers should not bypass family heads and reach into families for disciplinary or any other purposes. If they become aware of problems requiring discipline within a family, it is the family head that is to be consulted and/or disciplined as required. In this model, the family not only retains its integrity as a governing unit, but it is seen to be the initiating agency for the church as an institution.

The institutional church, governed by fallen men, is always subject to corruption. The Presbyterian system—a compromise between the excesses found in the highly centralized Episcopal and strictly local Congregational forms of church government—is probably the best choice possible, but it is not without problems. The many splits and resultant formations of new denominations (going back to the Reformation) attest to this fact. It has been primarily reactions from families and individuals that have restrained the corrupting influence of the power wielded by the few through these institutions. Do we really believe that today's denominations are that much better? Do we think that this intellectually poverty-stricken generation has the final answer? Or do we think that we can see progress in this long chain of experiments and that somewhere downstream the mature church will emerge victorious? If we are honest as well as perceptive, we must answer these questions no, no, and no.

A problem the church (the body of Christ) has been experiencing throughout its history is that to a great extent the individuals and families of which it is comprised, instead of accepting and assuming the responsibility God has placed upon them, have looked to an institution to do their work and their thinking for them. They have brought their tithes to the storehouse, laid them at the feet of their leaders, and gone about their business, content that they were faithful to the Great Commission. But Christ's commandments throughout the New Testament were addressed primarily to the body, not the institution. The use of the word "church" in Scripture is more often a reference to the body of Christ (i.e., a living spiritual organization of all believers) than it is to an institution. It is the godly, born-again, individual family head that is responsible for the building of the kingdom of God on earth. Yes, the institution is necessary and Biblically ordained, but it needs to be seen as a resource, a utility responsible to the families of the faithful. Its purity must be the concern of each member and kept constantly under guard.

Too many Christians today seem to believe that if they live godly lives, attend church services, and tithe, they are doing all that Christ requires of them. They don't feel burdened with the responsibility of building God's kingdom for two reasons. First, they have not been taught that it is their responsibility. This is no doubt the case because the men in the pulpit don't see it that way either. Second, they don't believe that victory is possible. They have been taught, again, by the ministers of the churches they attend, that the Christian faith will never command anything near a majority of the population and that true believers will forever remain a small remnant. Their prayer for God's kingdom to come is often something totally disconnected from the current world.

Because of the pessimism prevalent in modern theology, much of today's preaching is negative. Christians, not having the positive responsibility of building God's kingdom on earth, are taught to focus on controlling their tendencies toward sin. They must not do as the world does; they must defend themselves against Satan's attempts to subvert their faith, and they must work hard to remain pure for Christ. While these are good objectives, they are negative and hence difficult to maintain. A constant diet of such sermons is seemingly needed to keep the faithful in the faith. The loss of the positive goal of building God's kingdom has led to an apathetic attitude typical of individuals who have little or no responsibility in life. Many turn to other interests—interests outside the faith—to fill the vacuum in their lives.

Likewise, evangelism suffers. Because it fails to offer a significant goal and purpose for life in this world, it has only limited success, especially so with active, goal-oriented individuals. The world sees the church as irrelevant because it is irrelevant with respect to what is going on in the outside world. Membership roles and revenues shrink, but instead of taking a serious look at what the church is teaching and doing, it seems that too many church leaders tend to just multiply their recruiting efforts. They continue to fail but doggedly refuse to reconsider and critically reexamine any of their highly valued doctrines. In particular, it is pessimistic eschatology that is the principal cause:

One day all the nations of the world must submit to Christ! See Psalm 2:

> 1 Why do the heathen rage, and the people imagine a vain thing?
>
> 2 The kings of the earth set themselves, and the rulers take counsel together, against the LORD, and against his anointed, saying,
>
> 3 Let us break their bands asunder, and cast away their cords from us.
>
> 4 He that sitteth in the heavens shall laugh: the Lord shall have them in derision.
>
> 5 Then shall he speak unto them in his wrath, and vex them in his sore displeasure.
>
> 6 Yet have I set my king upon my holy hill of Zion.

7 I will declare the decree: the LORD hath said unto me, Thou art my Son; this day have I begotten thee.

8 Ask of me, and I shall give thee the heathen for thine inheritance, and the uttermost parts of the earth for thy possession.

9 Thou shalt break them with a rod of iron; thou shalt dash them in pieces like a potter's vessel.

10 Be wise now therefore, O ye kings: be instructed, ye judges of the earth.

11 Serve the LORD with fear, and rejoice with trembling.

12 Kiss the Son, lest he be angry, and ye perish from the way, when his wrath is kindled but a little. Blessed are all they that put their trust in him.

This is a psalm that declared what is *now* Christ's present reign and ultimate victory over all the currently rebellious nations and peoples of the world. The heathen are given to Him as His inheritance. In other words, they will eventually be converted to the Christian faith. The Lord laughs at every attempt to overthrow Christ's reign. The church must believe God, uphold this statement, and declare not just the *possibility* but the *certainty* of the ultimate victory, in time and in history, of God's people. Without this, hope is destroyed, people become discouraged, and victory is deferred.

Faith or Hypocrisy

The first requirement is faith; without faith there can be no victory. John tells us, "this is the victory that overcometh the world, even our faith" (see 1 John 5:4). The faith that John wrote of here is the same faith James referred to when he wrote in the second chapter:

17 Even so faith, if it hath not works, is dead, being alone.

18 Yea, a man may say, Thou hast faith, and I have works: show me thy faith without thy works, and I will show thee my faith by my works.

19 Thou believest that there is one God; thou doest well: the devils also believe, and tremble.

20 But wilt thou know, O vain man, that faith without works is dead?

True faith is a faith that is validated by deeds. Any so-called faith that is not supported by deeds commensurate with that statement of faith is false, a lie, or, as James says, "dead." This kind of dead faith is very prevalent in the world today, even among nominal Christians. Many of today's churches abound with people who consider themselves Christians but whose faith amounts to nothing more than an empty shell. It is true that John wrote "Whosoever shall confess that Jesus is the Son of God, God dwelleth in him, and he in God" (see 1 John 4:15). But does this mean that anyone who calls himself a Christian must be taken to be such?

To appreciate the significance of what John wrote here, we must recognize that it came in a time when to make such a confession could easily cost one his life. In that environment, the confession itself was sufficient proof of its truth. The situation today is quite different; to just say one believes is no longer a sufficient proof of faith. The words roll off the lips with apparent sincerity but often without any real depth of commitment or hope. Their lives are not changed by the faith they profess. The Bible is taken with a grain of salt as if it were good advice to be followed whenever it was convenient to do so. A sad statistic (though probably not true for committed Christians) often cited for many years is that the divorce rate in the "Christian community" is no different from that of the general public. No different? When God says that He hates divorce and they swore before God to love, honor, and cherish until death do us part!

Faith in Scripture is not merely belief; James tells us that "devils believe and tremble" (James 2:19). Paul tells us "the just shall live by faith" (Rom. 1:17; Gal. 3:11; Heb. 10:38). This is usually taken to mean that one is saved by faith, but the text speaks of life, which includes, but is broader than, salvation. The point is that salvation is only promised to those that carry their faith into the way they live their lives. The *just* or the *justified* are those whose faith is such that it is reflected into the way they live! Any so-called faith that falls short of this standard is not true faith. It does not come from the heart but is of a superficial nature and cannot govern one's actions as true faith does.[38]

---

38 For a more thorough description of true faith, see: R. J. Rushdoony, *Romans and Galatians*. Vallecito, CA: Ross House Books, 1997, 6–10.

Christ spoke of people who take His name—call themselves Christians —but fail to obey God's commandments in Matthew chapter 7:

> 21 Not every one that saith unto me, Lord, Lord, shall enter into the kingdom of heaven; but he that doeth the will of my Father which is in heaven.
>
> 22 Many will say to me in that day, Lord, Lord, have we not prophesied in thy name? and in thy name have cast out devils? and in thy name done many wonderful works?
>
> 23 And then will I profess unto them, I never knew you: depart from me, ye that work iniquity.

These are some of the most fearful and damning words in all of Scripture and, from all appearances today, there will be many that hear them. They will plead their sincerity and beg for mercy but will not receive it. They are condemned because they "work iniquity," i.e., they transgress God's law.

So, our first responsibility is to see to ourselves and ascertain the validity of our own faith. Is it a faith that would stand up to the kind of test James had in mind? Would we be willing to give up our lives rather than deny our faith? Really? Do we see ourselves as not our own but as bond-slaves of Christ, having been bought with a price?

When we have assured ourselves that such is the case, we need to consider how to relate to these unbelievers that have flooded our churches. It is not a simple question; some of these may well be elect of God that have not yet been born again. Others may be true Christians who are not very far along in the process of sanctification. We should remember that we also are still far from perfect; we're still undergoing redemptive change ourselves. It is clearly wrong to be overly judgmental and critical. Yet it also seems wrong somehow to just put our differences aside and pretend that everything's OK.

Most Christians leave it up to the pastor to provide the necessary criticism in a general way via sermons from the pulpit. While these can be a positive good, they are often not sufficient to deal with the problem. Too many pastors, having an eye to attendance and collections, are willfully negligent in their duty, which is to make these persons uncomfortable in their disobedience to God. These pastors need the encouragement, support, and a measure of insistence from the true believers in the congregation that they properly carry out their duties.

Unbelief must not go unchallenged. Churchgoers that clearly are unbelievers need to be informed of where they stand. It may be far better, for both the unbelievers and the church body, that they not be in church than to think they belong to something they really have no part in. This, of course, is a very sensitive subject and must be handled with great care; not everyone has the discernment and skills needed to properly deal with it.

What must be avoided though is the kind of situation that prevails in many churches today where large segments of the attendees and members are seekers or clearly unbelievers. When such unbelievers become congregation members and are treated as if they were born-again believers, the church body loses the respect of the youth, new attendees, and other onlookers. The hypocrisy of it is evident to the world at large and Christianity loses ground. In an effort to increase its numbers, the church loses its vitality and actually shrinks rather than grows.

Church membership, especially voting membership, should be much more restricted than it is today. Paul cautions us in 1 Timothy 5:22: "Lay hands suddenly on no man, neither be partaker of other men's sins: keep thyself pure." While this is primarily directed to elders and deacons, it applies as well to church membership. The power to vote is the power to institute potentially radical changes and must not be granted without great care. Many churches have been destroyed by membership vote.

Historically, the church has been a place where the faithful meet together to refresh and strengthen themselves and each other for their warfare with the world. It has been described as God's armory, where Christians can go to heal their wounds, refurbish their weapons, and prepare themselves for the next battle. It is an essential institution, without which the struggle against the enemy cannot gain ground. It is vital that the church retain its purity. It cannot function as the Lord intended when it is encumbered with large numbers of unregenerate members.

Prayer

Because of the frequent mention of prayer in Scripture and the fact that our Lord while He was on earth spent much time in prayer, we know that prayer is important. It is necessary for the creature to stay in contact with his Creator, but why? Why should Christians pray? Most prayer is in the form of petition, requests made of God for support with problems that arise in our lives. But God, before we begin to pray, already knows what we have need of and what we will ask. So why tell Him what He already knows? The question disappears when we realize that petition is not for God's benefit but for our own. We need to keep reminding ourselves: first, of our responsibilities before God; and second, that God is really in control of all events that transpire on earth. Prayer provides these necessary reminders.

Prayer also keeps us aware of the needs of those we pray for so that we remain diligent to do all we can to satisfy those needs to the extent we can. This connection between prayer and action is very significant. To pray for something within one's reach and then fail to take action to work toward it is hypocritical. It says that the prayer was disingenuous. If it were sincere, effort should have been exerted to try to bring about the thing prayed for, as we are able.

The prayer the Lord gave us in Matthew 6 is the model we should follow in all our prayers:

> 9 After this manner therefore pray ye: Our Father which art in heaven, Hallowed be thy name.
>
> 10 Thy kingdom come. Thy will be done in earth, as it is in heaven.
>
> 11 Give us this day our daily bread.
>
> 12 And forgive us our debts, as we forgive our debtors.
>
> 13 And lead us not into temptation, but deliver us from evil: For thine is the kingdom, and the power, and the glory, for ever. Amen.

This prayer begins first of all with God and His kingdom on earth. This tells us that His kingdom should be in the forefront of our minds, not just when we pray but always. To see His name hallowed should be a high priority in our lives. We should be disturbed when His name is taken in vain or trampled underfoot as a curse word.

The next two petitions are related; we are to be concerned with the establishment of His kingdom and obedience to His rule, first in our own lives and then in the world at large. To restrict this to a personal application, as many do today, is to violate the sense of the text. "Thy will be done in earth" means the whole earth, not just self or a select few. These petitions remind us of our own responsibility in the Great Commission.

It is only at the fourth petition that we begin to see requests for personal needs. "Give us this day our daily bread" helps us remember that it is God who provides for our every need and keeps us from self-satisfaction in our own efforts to do so. "Forgive us our debts (trespasses), as we forgive our debtors" reminds us of our responsibility to love our neighbor as ourselves. "Lead us not into temptation, but deliver us from evil" reminds us of our tendency to sin and our dependence on God who controls whatsoever comes to pass. "For thine is the kingdom, and the power, and the glory, for ever" encourages us to continue to fight against evil because God's power assures us that victory is certain.

Here again we can see the great emphasis God places on our responsibilities as His chosen people. The building of His kingdom must be the highest priority on our prayer list and the thing we must seek for with diligence. We have the privilege of being the instruments God has chosen to work His wonder-working power through in order to change lives. God effectually calls, and we sow and reap. Much more could be said about this prayer, but these particulars are almost always overlooked and need to be given due attention today.

CHRISTIAN RESPONSIBILITY

The responsibilities God gives man are not artificial or superficial but are real and significant. Man was always given work to do. Adam was not permitted to merely sit and bask in the sunlight of a completed creation. His responsibility included the completion of God's creative work. God left much for him to do and the same is true for Christians today. The world is to be Christianized by man without God doing it for him. God did not do the work He assigned to Adam, and Christ will not do the work He assigned to Christians. It has not been completed these two thousand years—and may require thousands more—but one day it will be done; and it will be done by man.

There is certainly no Scriptural warrant for the church as an institution to forsake the tenets of its basic charter in favor of social programs. But there is a great need for Christians as private citizens to do whatever they can, within their scope of authority and responsibility, to first combat the current slide into a humanistic culture, and then to rebuild the world to bring it into conformity with God's standards. In a godly society, many are born again. In a godless society, few, if any, are born again. Even though it is God who chooses His elect, man is still responsible to provide an environment conducive to the process. This is an example of the Biblical principle of the consistency of God's sovereignty with man's responsibility—a concept that goes beyond all human understanding. Christians must see to it that their children are taught in God-fearing schools. When they fail to do so, each generation becomes less and less godly because there are fewer and fewer Christians. The lack of recognition of this responsibility has been a prime factor in the decline of Christianity.

We all have eligibility to vote and a sphere of influence and positions with some level of authority, at least in the sense of advising those who look to us as leaders, and we are therefore responsible to provide good and godly advice and to take appropriate action. Is this not what Christ commanded us to do when He identified us as the light of the world and the salt of the earth? Is it not the lesson we should learn from the parable of the Good Samaritan? There is a suffering world out there that is descending into hell by the millions. Should we not offer them succor and aid to the extent we are able? Without God, they cannot govern themselves and will just continue to move farther and farther away from Him.

Today's Americans were born and raised in a reasonably Christian culture. We had the benefit of at least the form of godliness in our schools. The churches were open to us without the kinds of restraints common in communist and Muslim countries, restraints that are rapidly developing here as well. The entertainment world was not free and licensed to broadcast the ungodly messages that now pour into our living rooms. Were these not contributing factors that led to our conversion? How many of us would now be Christians had we been exposed in our youth to even today's culture, much less that of openly God-hating countries? Yes, God chooses and saves His elect, but we are the instruments He uses to accomplish His foreordained purposes. When we fail to obey Him in this, we become responsible for the many that are lost because they lacked the benefits our forebears blessed us with.

Or do we believe that there is no use trying? Is Satan so strong and Christ so weak that we should despair of ever obtaining any kind of victory? Many Christian churches are teaching just this sort of doctrine today and many Christians have moved over to the sidelines because of it. When they begin to see that this is not Biblical teaching, this will change and the recovery process will begin. We as the recipients of God's mercy and grace are His responsible agents. The fields are white and ready to harvest; there is a whole world out there desperately in need of God and God's law. It is time for us to awaken from our slumber, roll up our sleeves, and get busy with the task He has assigned us.

The Ongoing Struggle

The key question of course is which faith will win, Christianity or humanism? Will the world end up dominated by good or by evil? Christianity has had a strong hand and made great progress throughout the West for much of last two millennia, but false teachers, primarily located within the church, have led the woman's seed (true Christians) astray. They have been deceived into believing that they cannot win, that the forces of Satan are too strong and cannot be overcome without direct intervention by God Himself. They have also been taught that God's word predicts that, in history, Satan will be victorious and will defeat the church. As a consequence, Christians have withdrawn from the struggle, retreated into their church-oriented, citadel-like environments, and allowed the enemy to assume control of virtually every aspect of society at large. But the recent ascendance of the forces of evil is not the outworking of an irresistible, predetermined fate that cannot be altered. It is simply the consequence of a self-fulfilling prophecy. When an army is convinced it cannot win, it will not win.

But that doesn't mean it's all over, that Christians have lost and might as well just quit and go home. God, who knows the end from the beginning, has told us repeatedly that evil cannot last—the meek *will* inherit the earth and righteousness *will* reign supreme. God's laws govern the universe and to resist them is utter foolishness. This is true in the social world as well as the physical. Rebellion against God constitutes a flight from what is real. God's Word defines reality and the further one moves away from that word, the further he moves away from reality. We cannot have an enduring civilization that is governed by laws that violate those given by God.

Because they deny God's universal laws, today's godless governments cannot build or advance but are destined to destroy themselves. As this process develops, governments become irrational. We can see many aspects of this degradation at work in America today. This country is in moral and financial peril, wasting its resources in utterly foolish actions both at home and abroad and refusing to deal with real issues such as mounting debt, a weak and faltering economy, moral decline, lawlessness, and abortion. Christians today need to assert the truth of their faith and lift up God's law as the only rational basis for civil law. If they fail to do so and our leaders continue to move away from Christian government, the irrational behavior will intensify and the U.S. will very likely experience financial collapse and cease to be a world power. Should such be the case, recovery will be delayed to another generation, possibly to another country.

God has given Christians several opportunities to put the past behind and begin anew with a fresh start. Adam had a clear path, a whole new world to develop when he started. Noah also was given a clean slate; all unbelievers were removed with the flood. Abraham and then Moses were given a family-nation, a new land of their own, and God's law to guide them. Today, with Christ, things are somewhat different. In these last days, God sent His Son and there may not be any more resets and restarts. He has imbued His people with the power of the Holy Spirit, which is sufficient to fully carry out all God's purposes. Two thousand years have elapsed since Christ came and defeated Satan. How much longer will it be before a faithful generation arises and completes the work He has assigned to His church, His body? We don't know how many more generations must pass, but we can be sure God's kingdom will come and one day His will *will* be done—on earth as it is in heaven.

Impact

In the first few centuries of its history, the church impacted society in a very real sense. The people of that day related to the message and responded positively. This is not the case today. Unbelievers (at least for now) are quite content when we sit in comfortable churches and preach to one another. They rant and howl when we attempt to put God's laws on the books and apply it to the culture. When the churches respond by backing off, putting on a smiling face, and attempting to get on their good side, unbelievers recognize them for the hypocrites they are and appropriately despise and reject them. Attempts at evangelism are ordinarily successful only with the young and emotionally susceptible people. Perceptive individuals see church programs as irrelevant to their concerns and serving no earthly good. Consequently, they summarily reject weak and shallow church expression.

When they see a serious and consistent attempt by believers to change society for the better, most unbelievers are driven to anger and opposition; but some, even many, led by the Spirit, will give the Gospel message a hearing it would not otherwise have obtained. Instead of reducing, it would augment and expand the church's evangelistic outreach. More would come to church to better understand what is being taught, and why Christians are so adamant about applying God's word to the culture. Some might come out of enmity, and then persecution would surely increase. Yet, is that not the subsistence on which the church has thrived since its inception?

But how many of God's people are willing to suffer for their faith these days? Too many have grown fat and lazy, and, as Francis Schaeffer put it, are only interested in the continuance of the "personal peace and prosperity"[39] they currently enjoy. But it will not continue. Satan seeks to wipe out every trace of the faith from the face of the earth. He cannot succeed, but he will try. As long as Christians fail to resist him, he will continue to prevail. James enjoins us to "resist the devil, and he will flee" from us (4:7). This should be taken at the cultural as well as personal level. God assures us of victory (see Isa. 25:8; 1 Cor. 15:57), in time and in history, when we obey Him regardless of the consequences.

Christians will not impact society nor be successful evangelistically until they move away from the other-worldly spiritual image they now portray and begin to address the real temporal problems that concern people. The proclamation of the Gospel—in today's limited sense—should not be curtailed; but neither should it be the totality of what is preached.

The world situation as it exists today cannot be sustained; it is moving inexorably toward a collapse. When this time approaches, Christians

---

39 Francis A. Schaeffer, *How Should We then Live: The Rise and Decline of Western Thought and Culture.* Grand Rapids, MI: Fleming H. Revell Co., 1976, 246.

need to be ready to step in with the answers a desperate world will be looking for. The answers can only come from God, and His people need to be ready to supply them. The sooner a true Christian center of Biblical knowledge[40] is established and becomes well known, one that faithfully interprets God's word as the only answer to every question, the less pain will be felt during the recovery process.

At this writing, the American people are beginning to wake up to what their Federal government is doing to them. They are coming to the realization that both their liberties and their property are being eroded against their wishes and are making their voices heard at town hall meetings and other gatherings. Sadly though, the Christian churches and leaders are not at the forefront of this movement. It is the secular element that is taking the lead and Christians are following. This incongruous situation is an indication of how far the churches have strayed from Biblical teaching. The Black Robe Regiment,[41] pastors of the eighteenth century who led the struggle for independence, would not have approved of such shameful inaction.

God's Law

Until the culture is brought into line with God's word, like-minded Christians need to strive and also support one another in resisting the pernicious influence of non-Christian and wrong-Christian thinking in their personal lives. This is primary, but concurrent with this, they must continue to exert their influence toward the establishment of God's law in the culture at large. This should be done forthrightly and openly by declaring God's law to be the law above all laws. Even when it becomes unpopular, we must not shrink from this task. Christ told us we must expect hatred and opposition from the world (see John 15:18–25).

In today's world, this is not yet apparent. The antithesis God placed between the two seeds is not clearly delineated; the line is very blurred and indistinct. But as Christians begin to obey God in a fuller sense, the differences will become more apparent and the hatred of the world

---

40 Chalcedon Foundation, Vallecito, California may represent the beginning of such a center. It has the necessary theological basis but needs support to insure it will continue.

41 Black Robe Regiment: http://blackroberegiment.wallbuilders.com/the-original-brr/what-is-the-black-robed-regiment.aspx.

will also become more intense and more widespread. It is important for Christians to restrain from blurring the line through compromise or concession. The choice between good and evil must be clarified so that each individual decision can be made in a fully self-conscious manner. When the lines between good and evil are clearly drawn, self-deception becomes difficult and people are forced to really make a choice as to which they will serve. This, without doubt, would result in a thinning of the ranks, but the Lord's army would be strengthened and the faith would be advanced. As people become epistemologically self-conscious, and good and evil become more clearly distinguished, more and more Christians will begin to see that God's Law-Word must be obeyed in every particular of their life and cannot be dealt with through compromise or lip service.

We see this just beginning to take shape in the abortion controversy today, but there is still far too much uncertainty introduced by Christians who are trying to get help from the other side through compromises, such as, for example, exceptions for rape and incest. In an attempt to try to get some help from unbelievers, we allow the murder of the innocent in a few special cases. In doing so, we tell the world that God's Law-Word is not absolute; we can modify or abridge it as needed to suit particular circumstances.

Apart from the utter wrong-headedness involved here, we need to see that when we compromise God's word, we dishonor God. Any compromise smooths the path to the next concession. But more importantly, it undermines the authority of God's word in the view of the world. It lowers its status from a law-word to tidbits of potentially good advice, and this is the last thing we want to see happen.

Christians must realize that this work is not reserved, or even primarily applicable, to pastors, preachers, and theologians. Their work is the church, the teaching ministry, and the exposition of God's word. It is the responsibility of every Christian to uphold the Christian faith in every aspect of life. If Christ is Lord, then He is Lord over the church, the school, the place of business, the media, civil government, and every walk of life. If we believe that Christ is truly King of kings and Lord of lords, we must uphold Him as Lord of *all* and not limit His lordship to the Sunday church service and our personal lives.

Christians cannot win the culture for Christ if those who compose the body of Christ hide their lights under bushel baskets as so many do today. To look at the example of the abortion controversy once again, the arguments against abortion must reside primarily on God's law and not other considerations such as health or psychology. These considerations may be employed, but only as secondary aspects of the problem, not in place of the declaration of the supremacy of God's law over man's law. To do so is equivalent to saying there is no law from God. Sadly, because of defective theology, this is exactly what most of today's churches teach.

The early Christians, in an extremely hostile environment, said, "We ought to obey God rather than men" (see Acts 5:29). And in Acts 4:12, we read Peter's astounding declaration: "Neither is there salvation in any other: for there is none other name under heaven given among men, whereby we must be saved."

This highly political statement flew in the face of the Roman powers that saw and upheld Caesar as the savior of all men. The conflict these early believers had with Rome was not basically religious in nature; Rome saw it as political. In the Roman Empire, the only name under heaven whereby men were saved was the name of Caesar and to name another name is his place was tantamount to treason. Rome was willing to accept any religious faith so long as it left their state religion intact, that Caesar was lord in this world. The Christian insistence that Christ is lord over all was intolerable to them. They felt that, if Christianity was permitted public expression, it would lead to a complete breakdown of Caesar's authority and so Christianity could not be allowed to develop. The Roman persecution of those early Christians was not done just for religious reasons, but also because they were seen as a disruptive element in the political order of the day, as indeed they were, having eventually displaced it altogether.

Such public declaration of God's law as the higher law is not optional for Christians. Without it, the faith will decline rather than grow. It is in decline now and humanism is in ascension for this reason. No faith can dominate a culture without a law that represents that faith. All laws are religious in nature. The law of a nation is the religion of that nation applied to the civil life of that nation. One can see the faith of a people in the laws they enact. For Christians to cease the public declaration of God's law as the supreme law is for them to relinquish Christ's Great Commission. It is equivalent to "I surrender" in a time of war. But if we believe that Christ said He would be with us "even unto the end of the world" (see Matt. 28:20), how can we surrender to evil? He will keep His promise, and, if we persevere and continue in obedience to Him, victory will be ours.

THEOLOGY

The formula for victory is contained within the pages of Holy Scripture; but if through defective interpretation or defective theology we distort or discard much of what it says, we cannot expect to realize anything resembling success. We will be truly victorious to the extent we are truly obedient, by faith, and no more. We cannot expect God's blessing when we, through our theology, narrow His word down to approximate something we may be more comfortable with but which does not properly reflect its intent. Much of God's law seems uncomfortable to us but only because we approach it with presuppositions derived from the culture that surrounds us. When we suppress this tendency and examine God's word by God's standards, we can begin to see the depth of wisdom, love, and beauty in each and every commandment of God.

It is very difficult to give up something you've believed most or all of your life. We all develop a base of personal knowledge. To this pool we add everything we learn and remember throughout our lives. Because this process requires a lot of time and effort, this investment becomes dear to us; it is our treasure hoard and we resist giving up any of it. But a truly wise and honest person will realize that it can't all be correct. The truly wise and honest person will admit he is not a god unto himself but is a fallible, sinful, and very limited creature and never perfect in anything he does. Such a person is willing to review his knowledge base to see if he can improve on it. Even more important than acquiring new knowledge is the elimination of wrong ideas that have crept in over time. If we refuse to root out those things that need rooting out, we cannot make progress in our efforts to increase our knowledge and approach truth. None of us are perfect; indeed we are all very far from a thorough understanding of God's reality and need to see that any wrong ideas we hold to are a constant roadblock impeding growth in understanding. I implore the reader to set aside his pride and open his mind to what might be a different way of looking at God's word—but one that he might find most rewarding and highly worthwhile.

Much of today's popular theology, such as antinomianism, dispensationalism, pessimistic eschatologies, and man-centered soteriology (the theology of salvation) needs to be jettisoned. It must be replaced by the kind of sound Biblical teaching found today only in a very few places. This volume is far from sufficient to the task of doing so; it can only point to the fact that there are problems and where some of the difficulties lie. For a thorough and Biblically sound theological foundation, I recommend that the serious reader look into the Christian Reconstruction movement founded and championed by the late R. J. Rushdoony, and now capably led by his son, Mark Rushdoony. His very extensive work and that of his cohorts and successors can be found online at www.chalcedon.edu.

The notion of Christian Reconstruction is that, because we have drifted so far away from God's word, every institution of man needs to be reexamined from top to bottom using Biblical standards and then restructured as necessary along godly lines. This reconstruction program is most especially needed in the churches and seminaries, many of which have drastically distorted Scripture and led the nation and the world down some very wrong paths. This is not a new thing and should not lead us into discouragement; the pages of Christian history are filled with instances of doctrinal decline and recovery, the Reformation being one notable example. This too will pass, and recovery will ensue.

God is yet in control and will in His good time guide His people into all truth and eventually He will right all wrongs. First and foremost, the Lord Jesus Christ, the Alpha and Omega, initiates His power working through His flock, the church. This means that recovery must start with common individual Christians, not with some highly visible, charismatic leaders. Chalcedon and other organizations can be supporters and resource centers but not the initiators and implementers of the process. Each person, acting in obedience to God, influences the people around him. The circles grow and eventually coalesce until the entire culture is converted.

12

OUTCOMES

How, though, is simple obedience to God the path to victory for Christianity? Humanism clearly has the upper hand all over the world today. We are no longer where we were in the America of the eighteenth century when Christianity dominated the culture. How can just obeying God give us victory over the enormous power of entrenched humanism? There are two things that need to be considered here:

THE OPPOSITION

First, humanism (in its modern atheistic sense)—the primary alternative to Christianity in the world today—cannot produce a workable social system. It is contrary to man's basic nature and carries within itself the seeds of its own destruction. To look at just one of the many deficiencies present in a humanistic society, let's consider its economy. Since in that system there is no transcendental God and no law of God to govern individuals from within, the only law available is man's law, which, as we saw above, is dependent on forced compliance and therefore is incompatible with individual freedom. But without freedom, initiative dies, production is drastically reduced, and the whole system, being economically and hence politically unsustainable, eventually collapses. Today, because of the ameliorating effect of Christianity, this is not readily observable. Most civilized people, even unbelievers, are still largely governed by Christian principles and do what is right without realizing it. This dilutes the humanism in a humanistic society and delays the consequences that it produces. The Western world has never seen a fully consistent humanistic society and has never experienced its consequences. Soviet Russia was probably the closest to such a society in modern times but even there mitigating factors were present. It was not truly isolated from the Christian nations that surrounded it and the traditions and morays of its previous Christian society had not fully faded away. Although it began with a very well-developed economy and considerable natural resources, it collapsed after only two generations.

People today don't appreciate the extent to which our culture has been influenced by a tradition of faith in God. Even unbelievers have a sense of right and wrong that's based on the religious notions of their forebears and the surrounding culture. These ethics come from the Bible and possess a great deal of inertia. The ideas of right and wrong are not easily changed; they continue through generation after generation losing or gaining strength depending on the degree of influence, or lack thereof, of the Christian faith. Moral values have lost ground and diminished considerably over the past two centuries, but a great deal still remain.

Humanism, though, if fully implemented, would erode this sense of right and wrong much more rapidly. It would be considerably worse than paganism, which at least had gods of a sort, gods that people were careful not to offend. Given totally free rein, man's innate selfishness would eventually so dominate his character that virtually all trust between individuals would be lost. In such a situation, self-government degrades to self-service, leading to ever-increasing lawlessness, which in turn leads to an ever-increasing use of force in an attempt to maintain civil order. These two factors, lack of trust and the accompanying increase in man-made laws, regulations, and red tape, taken together would eventually so disrupt the division of labor that the national free-enterprise economy could not be sustained. The extremely high standard of living found in the Western world is based on both technological development and the high degree of specialization associated with the extremely fine-tuned and extensive division of labor in their economies. But the latter is dependent on trust and the freedom from government interference that trust makes possible. When trust is lost, the division of labor and the economy shrink and everyone is poorer.

Indeed, at the time of this writing, humanism is already beginning to show signs of serious internal disarray. Today's humanistic world order is well into the disintegration process. This is evident from the refusal of the world's governments to recognize or take any action to correct the hugely excessive debt loads they are carrying. They see that they are headed for financial collapse but are powerless or unwilling to avoid the coming calamity. From all appearances, they pretend that nothing is wrong. We are left to wonder if they think perhaps, somehow, something will happen to fix the problem while they continue to increase the debt, pushing the problem into the next administration or onto the next generation.

Second, we are seeing what appear to be spontaneous popular uprisings around the world reflecting a general dissatisfaction with the way that the Islamic form of humanistic government deals with citizens. The common people in these dictatorial countries are resorting to violent demonstrations to gain the freedom they see in the West. Islam is not the irresistible power some think. Iran, its center, has been thoroughly infected with western technology, particularly the Internet, which displays the contrast between East and West. The time will come, perhaps fairly soon, when the governments throughout Islam will not be able to suppress the popular will. This godless religion, that has been a thorn in the side of Christianity for centuries, will finally collapse of its own weight. Humanism in all its forms, while apparently strong today, is failing everywhere and will continue to fail until eventually it fails completely.

———

The level of civilization and prosperity we enjoy in the Western world today is an outgrowth of the centuries of Christianity that preceded it. As this influence continues to diminish and the trust and freedom it engenders diminish with it, the wealth we now enjoy will erode further. People's confidence in government will sink to even lower levels and they will become more ready to listen to Christians that uphold God's law and offer it as an alternative. Indeed, there is no real alternative to God's law; were it to disappear entirely, the world would become a jungle where dog-eat-dog is the way of life for the few that survive.

Even if, by some diabolical stratagem, the current humanistic order was to grow stronger and manage to suppress all expression of Christianity, even if it takes total control of all the earth's cultures, the result will be the same: Humanism will eventually collapse of its own weight and the Christian faith will revive. Christianity will rise up from the ashes of whatever level of destruction humanism might inflict upon the world. This cycle may be repeated any number of times, but eventually we will learn that humanism is not the way, and a sufficiently strong, God-fearing society will arise to establish a lasting, truly Christian order. This must be so because Christianity will never be eliminated and humanism must always fail. It cannot sustain itself, even in the absence of Christian resistance.

So humanism is not what it purports itself to be and it cannot continue without the support of the lingering Christianity it currently leans on. It has wreaked a great deal of havoc and damage throughout the world, but it has feet of clay and foreshadows only collapse and death for its future. Remember the words of the Lord from Proverbs 8:36: "all they that hate me love death." This hatred of life that characterizes humanism assures its eventual demise.

GOD'S POWER

We must not forget that God is in control of everything that happens in this world. Martin Luther's hymn (1529), "A Mighty Fortress Is Our God," assesses the situation very accurately.

Of Satan he said:

> For still our ancient foe
> Doth seek to work us woe;
> His craft and power are great,
> And, armed with cruel hate,
> On earth is not his equal.

> Did we in our own strength confide,
> Our striving would be losing. . . .

And of God, Luther said:

> And though this world, with devils filled,
> Should threaten to undo us,
> We will not fear, for God hath willed
> His truth to triumph through us:
> The prince of darkness grim,

We tremble not for him;
His rage we can endure,
For lo! his doom is sure,
One little word shall fell him.

Today, as in Luther's day, the power of the Prince of Darkness seems immense, overwhelming, and undefeatable. It's easy in such a situation to tremble and want to give up and stop trying; it is easy to forget that God is still in control and that Satan had to get permission from God before he could touch Job. The God of Joshua, of Gideon, of David, and of many faithful Israelites of old still reigns and will do as He wills.

God has promised blessings and victory to His people when they are faithful and obey His law. Also, as was demonstrated in the case of Gideon, numbers don't matter; God can give victory to three hundred against tens of thousands. He can also cause the numbers of the faithful to increase to however many are needed to accomplish His purposes. Where there are two or three together in His name, there is present with them the greatest force the world has ever seen (see Matt. 18:20). There is no limit to what can be accomplished, no limit to the extent God can shower down His blessings on His obedient children. The key word here is obedience, total obedience, obedience without reservations or restrictions; lack of obedience, disobedience, brings down His curses instead of blessings.

Satan's power is great today because Christians have been disobeying God and God is using Satan and His emissaries on earth as His rod to chastise His wayward people. We seem to be facing an invincible enemy; but, the truth is, it is our own disobedience that continually defeats us. Hal Lindsey's book, *Satan Is Alive and Well on Planet Earth*, is not the final word. According to the Word of God, Jesus wins on earth, as in Heaven. When we turn back to God's word and take it to heart as our Law-Word, Satan's power will diminish greatly and he will seem much less formidable as an opponent. Obedience redirects God's power in our favor. We should also appreciate that, more often than not, God's power works through His people. Often to our great surprise, the actions we take as we obey God, without any apparent divine intervention, directly bring about the desired result.

FAITH ON EARTH?

So let us come back to the question Christ raised: "Shall there be faith on earth when I return?" Was He questioning whether there would be any faith at all remaining on earth? Or was the question rather, will the faith grow and prosper to the extent that it covers the whole earth? Is He asking: "Will my mandate be carried out as I have commanded? Will my chosen ones be faithful and complete their mission?" If you are a Christian, these questions are directed to you and me and we must answer, for the responsibility is ours.

With respect to this question, God's word is a source of comfort. It is replete with promises of a future time of great blessing under Christ's rule. Consider the following passages [*emphasis mine*]:

Numbers 14:

> 21 But as truly as I live, *all the earth* shall be filled with the glory of the LORD.

Psalm 72:

> 8 He shall have *dominion also from sea to sea*, and from the river *unto the ends of the earth*.

> 9 They that dwell in the wilderness shall bow before him; and his enemies shall lick the dust.

> 10 The kings of Tarshish and of the isles shall bring presents: the kings of Sheba and Seba shall offer gifts.

> 11 Yea, all kings shall fall down before him: *all nations shall serve him*.

Isaiah 11:

> 1 And there shall come forth a rod out of the stem of Jesse, and a Branch shall grow out of his roots:

> 2 And the spirit of the LORD shall rest upon him, the spirit of wisdom and understanding, the spirit of counsel and might, the spirit of knowledge and of the fear of the LORD;

> 3 And shall make him of quick understanding in the fear of

the LORD: and he shall not judge after the sight of his eyes, neither reprove after the hearing of his ears:

4 But with righteousness shall he judge the poor, and reprove with equity for the meek of the earth: and he shall smite the earth with the rod of his mouth, and with the breath of his lips shall he slay the wicked.

5 And righteousness shall be the girdle of his loins, and faithfulness the girdle of his reins.

6 The wolf also shall dwell with the lamb, and the leopard shall lie down with the kid; and the calf and the young lion and the fatling together; and a little child shall lead them.

7 And the cow and the bear shall feed; their young ones shall lie down together: and the lion shall eat straw like the ox.

8 And the sucking child shall play on the hole of the asp, and the weaned child shall put his hand on the cockatrice' den.

9 They shall not hurt nor destroy in all my holy mountain: *for the earth shall be full of the knowledge of the LORD*, as the waters cover the sea.

10 And in that day there shall be a root of Jesse, which shall stand for an ensign of the people; *to it shall the Gentiles seek*: and his rest shall be glorious.

Isaiah 45:

22 Look unto me, and *be ye saved, all the ends of the earth*: for I am God, and there is none else.

23 I have sworn by myself, the word is gone out of my mouth in righteousness, and shall not return, That *unto me every knee shall bow, every tongue shall swear.*

Jeremiah 31:

33 But this shall be the covenant that I will make with the house of Israel; After those days, saith the LORD, I will put my law in their inward parts, and write it in their hearts; and will be their God, and they shall be my people.

34 And they shall teach no more every man his neighbour, and every man his brother, saying, Know the LORD: *for they shall all know me,* from the least of them unto the greatest of them, saith the LORD: for I will forgive their iniquity, and I will remember their sin no more.

Daniel 7:

27 And the kingdom and dominion, and the greatness of the kingdom under the whole heaven, shall be given to the people of the saints of the most High, whose kingdom is an everlasting kingdom, and all dominions shall serve and obey him.

Micah 4:

1 But in the last days it shall come to pass, that the mountain of the house of the LORD shall be established in the top of the mountains, and it shall be exalted above the hills; and *people shall flow unto it.*

2 And many nations shall come, and say, Come, and let us go up to the mountain of the LORD, and to the house of the God of Jacob; and he will teach us of his ways, and we will walk in his paths: for *the law shall go forth* of Zion, and the word of the LORD from Jerusalem.

3 And he shall judge among many people, and rebuke strong nations afar off; and they shall beat their swords into plowshares, and their spears into pruninghooks: nation shall not lift up a sword against nation, neither shall they learn war any more.

4 But they shall sit every man under his vine and under his fig tree; and none shall make them afraid: for the mouth of the LORD of hosts hath spoken it.

Psalm 110:

1 The LORD said unto my Lord, Sit thou at my right hand, until I make thine enemies thy footstool.

2 The LORD shall send the rod of thy strength out of Zion: *rule thou in the midst of thine enemies.*

3 Thy people shall be willing in the day of thy power, in the beauties of holiness from the womb of the morning: thou hast the dew of thy youth.

4 The LORD hath sworn, and will not repent, Thou art a priest for ever after the order of Melchizedek.

5 The Lord at thy right hand shall strike through kings in the day of his wrath.

6 *He shall judge among the heathen,* he shall fill the places with the dead bodies; he shall wound the heads over many countries.

Ephesians 1:

19 And what is the exceeding greatness of his power to usward who believe, according to the working of his mighty power,

20 Which he wrought in Christ, when he raised him from the dead, and set him *at his own right hand* in the heavenly places,

21 Far above all principality, and power, and might, and dominion, and every name that is named, not only in this world, but also in that which is to come:

22 And hath *put all things under his feet,* and gave him to be the head over all things to the church,

Acts 2:

29 Men and brethren, let me freely speak unto you of the patriarch David, that he is both dead and buried, and his sepulchre is with us unto this day.

30 Therefore being a prophet, and knowing that God had sworn with an oath to him, that of the fruit of his loins, according to the flesh, he would *raise up Christ to sit on his throne;*

31 He seeing this before spake of the resurrection of Christ, that his soul was not left in hell, neither his flesh did see corruption.

32 This Jesus hath God raised up, whereof we all are witnesses.

33 Therefore being by the right hand of God exalted, and having received of the Father the promise of the Holy Ghost, he hath shed forth this, which ye now see and hear.

34 For David is not ascended into the heavens: but he saith himself, The LORD said unto my Lord, *Sit thou on my right hand,*

35 Until I make thy foes thy footstool.

1 Corinthians 15:

23 But every man in his own order: Christ the firstfruits; afterward they that are Christ's at his coming.

24 Then cometh the end, when he shall have delivered up the kingdom to God, even the Father; when he shall have *put down all rule and all authority and power.*

25 For he must reign, till he hath put *all enemies under his feet.*

Hebrews 10:

12 But this man, after he had offered one sacrifice for sins for ever, *sat down on the right hand of God;*

13 From henceforth expecting till his enemies be made his footstool.

Revelation 19:

11 And I saw heaven opened, and behold a white horse; and he that sat upon him was called Faithful and True, and *in righteousness he doth judge* and make war.

12 His eyes were as a flame of fire, and on his head were many crowns; and he had a name written, that no man knew, but he himself.

13 And he was clothed with a vesture dipped in blood: and his name is called The Word of God.

14 And the armies which were in heaven followed him upon white horses, clothed in fine linen, white and clean.

15 And out of his mouth goeth a sharp sword, that with it he should smite the nations: and *he shall rule them with a rod of iron:* and he treadeth the winepress of the fierceness and wrath of Almighty God.

16 And he hath on his vesture and on his thigh a name written, KING OF KINGS, AND LORD OF LORDS.

These verses and many, many others point to a future Christian world order, one that will come about while Christ sits at God the Father's right hand—*before* His second coming. He has completed the groundwork and sent His people, all that have been born of the Spirit, that share in His humanity, to complete the mopping up operation and bring the nations into submission to Him. They have been empowered by the Holy Spirit and will ultimately be victorious in their efforts.

God does not go back on His word and will perform today what He has promised in the past. How He will bring it about and how long it will take we cannot know, but bring it about He will. It may be in our time or it may be generations off, but this should be immaterial to us. What is important is that we do the work He has placed before us in our time. We have an eternity waiting and a task our God has given before us. Let us do as He has commanded and not be concerned with outcomes or time frames. God will give us victory, satisfaction, and blessings innumerable if only we are faithful and obedient. And if, for all our expenditure of effort, there is little or no progress made in our lifetime, what does it matter? If we continue in faithful obedience to our God, we can know we have done our part and will hear His blessing: "Well done, good and faithful servant; thou hast been faithful over a few things, I will make thee ruler over many things: enter thou into the joy of thy lord" (Matt. 25:23).

SCRIPTURE INDEX

About the Author

L ou Poumakis is a retired electrical engineer. He practiced this profession until his retirement in 2002 but has been a serious student of God's word since his conversion in 1974. He was ordained as elder in the Christian Reformed Church and later as minister in the Federation of Reformed Churches. Early on, he was attracted to the work of R. J. Rushdoony at Chalcedon Foundation where he discovered Postmillennialism and Christian Reconstruction. These doctrines reflected a truly Biblical Christian faith that possessed a dynamic that contrasted favorably with the passive outlook that predominated in what he had seen elsewhere. *Faith on Earth?* is primarily based on information garnered from this source. Before writing *Faith on Earth?*, he published several articles relating God's word to current events. He and his wife Joan, who have been married since 1955, now live in Florida. They have been blessed with two children, seven grandchildren, and three great-grandchildren.

PUBLISHER'S WORD

When the Son of man cometh,
shall he find faith on the earth?"

Luke 18:8

THE voluminous work of the late Dr. Rousas John Rushdoony, founder of Chalcedon Foundation, has remarkably influenced Biblical understanding in the twentieth-century church. The Nordskogs have long supported this work. Therefore, we are pleased to publish this important new contribution to Biblical worldview literature.

Faith on Earth? by Lou Poumakis crisply summarizes Dr. Rushdoony's applied Biblical faith in this readable and pithy overview. It begins with Christ's question, "When the Son of man cometh, shall he find faith on the earth?" (Lk. 18:8). Faith is a big term. Faith means understanding that God is our great Father, Lord, and Redeemer. Everything in life belongs to Him. In this world of ultimate spiritual battle for the souls of men, everything matters for God's glory and mankind's good. Otherwise, all must count toward sinful death and destruction. No territory is neutral. Faith requires the constant, thorough seeking of God, of His purposes, and His ways. Faith defers to God in all things—including everything economic and everything relational, even the civil sphere and its politics. The whole Bible is God's Law-Word, as all Scripture is inspired of God (2 Ti. 3:16).

For too long the church has allowed a misguided and essentially Greek view to direct Christian life. In this view, known historically as Pietism, only so-called spiritual things are good. Material things are evil. The Gnostics went so far in this regard as to characterize Satan as the hero of the creation story. He thus attempted to stop the Creator from creating an evil material universe. The common Christian version of this gnosticism, upon a limited Biblical understanding, teaches that the mysterious spiritual realm is the only good, Satan owns this world, and thus any

151

involvement in it, short of evangelizing, means soiling our spiritual selves. They believe salvation is essentially personal and irrelevant to the greater community. Often, a primary temporal goal of this faith is to find God in merely mystical experience. Such practice completely ignores the moral and ethical imperatives of the Gospel. Many varieties of this view have merged to become the mainstream Evangelical Movement. Added to it, Dispensationalism has provided a seeming rational excuse for allowing the world to go to ruin. In Dispensationalism, the world must become increasingly evil. As it reaches a crescendo of wickedness, Jesus will rapture His church from the world, and soon after will set up an external kingdom of Christ's rule-of-iron over the remnant of the evil world.

On the face of it, the Pietistic and Dispensational view flies in the face of the ministry of the Holy Spirit. Even Christ's disciples at first expected such an external Kingdom. But no. Christ's Kingdom expands from the heart of the individual outwards under the salt and light influence of believers. Thus, Jesus said the Kingdom comes without observation (Lk. 17:20). The Biblical view, the one the early American Pilgrims and Puritans held, says that Christ's ministry will successfully fill the world with a mountain (world order) made without hands (Dan. 2:35, 44–45). Psalm 110 indicates that Christ rules at the right hand of the Father, reigning in the midst of His enemies, until they are made His footstool (Mt. 22:44; 1 Co. 15:25-26; Heb. 2:8). Clearly, Christ intends to rule over an earthly Kingdom, in anticipation of eternity, by expanding His benevolent influence through His people as they build the Kingdom. He rules by His Holy Spirit through the individual hearts of those who belong to Him.

In *Faith on Earth?*, Lou Poumakis presents a Biblical worldview designed to bring us out of selfish Christianity into the Kingdom-oriented faith of the Scriptures. Lou does an excellent job of stimulating our thinking of the world on Christ's terms. The church and the yet to be

evangelized world need this message. When He returns in glory, may Christ indeed declare, "Yes, the Son of Man found faith on the earth!"

— Gerald Christian Nordskog,
Publisher
Christmas, 2012

To see all of our exciting titles and
view book contents, and to order ebooks
go to:
www.NordskogPublishing.com

If you like FREE *information*,
you are in for enjoyment, insight, and
inspiration via our **eNewsletter**.
Sign up here:
www.NordskogPublishing.com/eNewsletter

We also invite you to browse
many short articles, poems, and testimonies
by various perceptive writers.
To enjoy, go here:
PublishersCorner.NordskogPublishing.com

Ask the publisher about upcoming titles
and e-book versions, and a discount when
you purchase multiple books.